Integrity
in
Depth

Number Two
CAROLYN AND ERNEST FAY SERIES
IN ANALYTICAL PSYCHOLOGY
David H. Rosen, General Editor

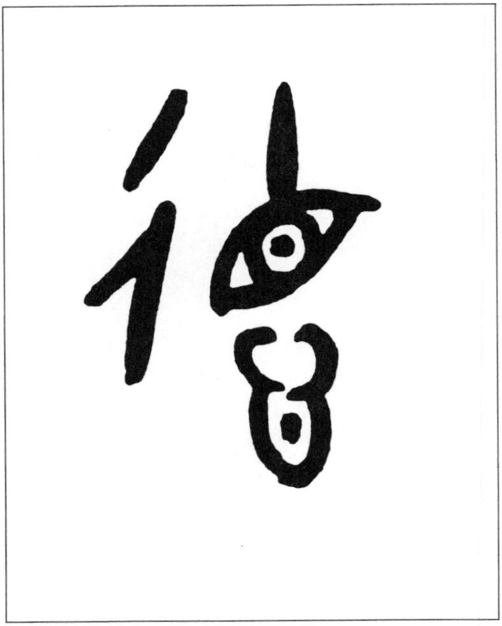

Integrity in Depth

John Beebe

FOREWORD BY DAVID H. ROSEN

Texas A&M University Press
College Station

The paper used in this book meets the minimum requirements
of the American National Standard for Permanence
of Paper for Printed Library Materials, Z39.48-1984.
Binding materials have been chosen for durability.

LIBRARY OF CONGRES CATALOGING-IN-PUBLICATION DATA
Beebe, John.
    Integrity in depth / John Beebe ; foreword by David H.
Rosen.
        p.   cm. — (Carolyn and Ernest Fay series in ana-
lytical psychology ; no. 2)
    Includes bibliographical references and index.
    ISBN 0-89096-493-9 (alk. paper)
      1. Shadow (Psychoanalysis)   2. Integrity.   I. Title.
II. Series.
BF175.5.S55B44   1992
155.2'32 — dc20   91-27214
                                CIP

Number Two
CAROLYN AND ERNEST FAY SERIES
IN ANALYTICAL PSCYHOLOGY
David H. Rosen, General Editor

The Carolyn and Ernest Fay edited book series, based initially on the annual Fay Lecture Series in Analytical Psychology, was established to further the ideas of C. G. Jung among students, faculty, therapists, and other citizens and to enhance scholarly activities related to analytical psychology. The Book Series and Lecture Series address topics of importance to the individual and to society. Both series were generously endowed by Carolyn Grant Fay, the founding president of the C. G. Jung Educational Center in Houston, Texas. The series are in part a memorial to her late husband, Ernest Bel Fay. Carolyn Fay has planted a Jungian tree carrying both her name and that of her late husband, which will bear fruitful ideas and stimulate creative works from this time forward. Texas A&M University and all those who come in contact with the growing Fay Jungian tree are extremely grateful to Carolyn Grant Fay for what she has done. The holder of the Frank N. McMillan, Jr. Professorship in Analytical Psychology at Texas A&M functions as the general editor of the Fay Book Series.

For Joseph Henderson

Contents

Foreword

*Nothing is at last sacred but the integrity of your own mind. Absolve
you to yourself, and you shall have the suffrage of the world.*
— EMERSON

JOHN BEEBE has successfully carried out an immense task of understanding one of the most challenging subjects: *integrity,* and
in depth! He has completed his archeological work extremely
well, excavating from the surface to the center, and we progress
through layers of philosophy, psychology, and literature, as well
as western and eastern spiritual disciplines. In the process, Dr.
Beebe uncovers innumerable elements that compose the whole.
Integrity comprises responsibility, uprightness, standing tall, being untouched, staying intact, completeness, perfection, honesty,
moral obligation, delight, inner psychological harmony, continuity, psychological and ethical eros, sincerity, chastity, virginity, obedience, conscience, prudence, purity, constancy, amiability, and holiness. And all this makes sense, because the definition
of integrity or *integritas* is the entire. Integrate and integration
come from the same Latin root as integrity. Integrate means to
combine all the disparate elements into one harmonious entity.
This is what Beebe does, and his labor of *integration* is an act of
renewing and restoring integrity. The circle is complete, and it
is meaningful that Beebe makes the connection of integrity with
the Self, which represents the center and the totality in Jung's
psychological system. Both integrity and the Self are spiritual concepts that unify and facilitate transcendence and transformation.

John Beebe was an instructor of mine at the C. G. Jung Institute in San Francisco; he was an accomplished teacher. This volume reveals that he is still teaching, but now his wise words come out of more years of clinical work and human experience. When Beebe first mentioned his title to me, it clicked. It was a natural because I had always thought of him as a person with integrity. Therefore, it does not surprise me to sense Beebe emerging from this work with enthusiasm, revealing that he has gone to the center and glimpsed the Self. He breaks through the surface of the water after his in-depth dive as an integrity-full person renewed.

John Beebe begins his book with "A Psychological Definition of Integrity," chapter 1. In the first section, he provides us with a map of the territory, in which we embark on an arduous journey to understand integrity, "to risk the mystery." We dive deep below the surface into unexplored waters. We focus on the supraordinate dimension of integrity, which parallels Jung's concept of the Self. Beebe posits that "integrity must be pursued as a desideratum in itself." He further states, "The implication is that the real pleasure in exercising integrity in dealings with others is the discovery of integrity itself." Beebe's maxim is similar to the well-known statement by Francis Peabody in medicine: "The secret of the care of the patient is in caring for the patient."

Beebe then develops the relationship between integrity and psychology, which he sees as linked through the Self. Discussing psychological types, he underscores that feeling is as significant as thinking, and intuition as important as sensation. Emphasizing the particular salience of intuition, Beebe states, "Intuition brings us a sense of the ecology of integrity, for intuition is the function that gives a feeling for the entire pattern operating in a given moment."

Beebe introduces Eastern spiritual concepts from the *I Ching* and *Tao Te Ching*. From the latter he principally focuses on *te,* which has been translated from the recently discovered Ma-wang-tui manuscripts as integrity by Victor H. Mair. Professor Mair was kind enough to send me a reproduction of an actual Chinese pictograph, which serves as the frontispiece of this book. It includes an eye looking straight ahead, the heart, and the sign for movement or behavior. The eye, symbolizing inner and outer vision, must be in harmony with the heart (feelings or soul), and with the movement or behavior of the person to determine if the individual's actions are integrity-full. After providing a map of the territory of integrity and an introduction to its psychological realm, Beebe then leads us into the darkest part of the journey.

Chapter 2 is titled "The Shadow and Integrity." It first focuses on the shadow. Beebe introduces the supposition that in our anxiety about the unknown other (the other within, the one that we project outside, or the other outside that causes anxiety inside) lies the actual field where the seeds of the shadow are planted. These grow into shadow plants that can be harvested, as this part of the book shows, yielding much food for thought. Beebe casts anxiety in a helpful way. For example, he tells us that "the signal is not wrong, it is telling us that our integrity is somehow at risk." After exploring the fertile ground of the shadow and how we can benefit by going into the scary realm of anxiety, he moves on to rediscover the Puritan Forefather in the next section. Through John Milton's poetry, Beebe challenges us to recapture some of the lost moral high ground of the Puritans. Milton had a conception of the education of integrity and, like Benjamin Franklin (who is discussed earlier in the book), lived a life of integrity.

In search of an archetypal image of integrity, Beebe turns to Marina Warner, who tells the story of Tuccia, a vestal virgin of Rome. Tuccia, accused of breaking her vow of chastity, proves how chaste she actually is by filling her sieve with water, which miraculously holds it. Tuccia's sieve, made whole by the power of her own wholeness, provides us with a symbol of ideal integrity. In many ways this symbolic image is like a Zen Koan. Beebe takes this intriguing symbol of the sieve from Warner's book *Monuments and Maidens.* He then makes a great leap forward in linking Tuccia's sieve with the "image of the analytic container, the ark of the psychotherapy relationship." Beebe adds, "Analytical psychotherapists have grown used to working within this closed but open space."

Other related metaphors come to mind, such as the cell, which on a microcosmic level is a contained whole system that has a permeable membrane. On a macrocosmic level, the earth also is a spherical entity that breathes and is alive. Like the psychotherapy relationship, both are intact, closed but open systems. Currently the earth is in danger from pollution and nuclear weapons and, as Jung claimed, we are the real danger. That's why Beebe's topic is so timely and of critical import. Beebe outlines three stages of integrity as related to the shadow: denial that there even is a shadow; a turning point that is the acceptance of the shadow; and a sense of restored wholeness, when the shadow has been integrated (here is that word again).

Beebe concludes this packed second chapter with a section he calls "Dialogue with Shame." He provocatively, but I think accurately, suggests that in addition to anxiety we will find integrity on the other side of shame. He suggests that we embrace shame, and his source for this wisdom is the *I Ching.* In an act of integrity, Beebe admits to the common problem of colluding with the attitude that shame is something to be ashamed of. He agrees with Andrew Morrison that for any individual with major deficits of the self, shame, not rage, is the principal affect. Beebe advocates "a psychology of healing through shame." He goes on to say that "such shame is healing only if it is held with integrity. The alchemical name for holding shame with integrity is *mortificatio,* the rot of human chemicals in a closed container—truly a mortifying experience." It occurs to me that Primo Levi's survival in Auschwitz and his reflections thereupon support Beebe's premise. In Levi's last book, *The Drowned and the Saved,* he even has a chapter on shame. It is clear that Primo Levi's integrity emerges out of mortification—out of the umbra of witnessing mechanized disgraceful mass beatings and killings of innocent men, women, and children.

Survival has to do with enduring and transcending obstacles, which is facilitated by the flame of hope, the bedrock of faith, a strong sense of self, and *integritas.* In fact, it is the virtue of hope that interrelates the first psychological issue (trust versus mistrust), the second (autonomy versus shame and doubt), and the last (integrity versus despair) in Erik Erikson's eight stages of human development. It is revealing that Erikson saw the otherwise stepwise and epigenetic stages in his developmental schema as becoming circular with the last and the first stages, with hope providing the spherical union. It seems to me that hope is the *temenos* (sacred place) for integrity.

Chapter 3, "Integrity and Gender," starts off with a section on "The Sensibility of Continuity," which relates to Jane Austen's work. Beebe links the practice of psychotherapy and the constancy of the process to the feminine receptive holding environment. Austen emphasized the unconscious wisdom of wholeness resulting in an image of the closed circle that parallels Jung's concept of the Self. Beebe stresses that the idea of wholeness, or unbroken continuity, has a central feminine virtue like a good mother. He emphasizes the similarity to "our modern idea of ecology, which has the Gaia hypothesis behind it."

After discussing integration through the anima, Beebe introduces a subtly differentiated post-Jungian view of gender. It draws upon Jung's alchemical conception of *sol* and *luna,* but as revised by Howard Teich. Teich sees solar and lunar not as gender principles in themselves, as Jung had done in equating sun with masculine and moon with feminine. Rather he approaches solar and lunar as psychological characteristics that can modify the expression of either gender. There is a lunar as well as solar masculinity, and a solar as well as lunar femininity. Although they are complicated, Beebe makes these concepts understandable. It seems to me that he ends up with something very like an ancient Yin/Yang view of wholeness in which the Yang (masculine) contains the feminine and the Yin (feminine) contains the masculine. Jung's image of the *coniunctio*, union of gender opposites — the same concept as conscious androgyny — is "our culture's strongest vision of moral wholeness," according to Beebe.

The fourth chapter of the book is "Working on Integrity." In its opening section, "Fidelity to Process," Beebe shares a poignant therapeutic interchange in which he makes a mistake that leads to the patient's being angry at him. This rage facilitates the patient's discovery of her own integrity and precedes Beebe's healing through shame and a renewal of his own integrity.

In the next section, "The Paradoxical Dream," Beebe postulates "that monitoring integrity is one of the chief functions of the dream, and that it ought to guide the way we look at dreams and the way we work with them." He shares a patient's very brief dream regarding a bottle cap that leads to the termination of therapy as well as the patient's marriage and job. This is a clear and amazing example of the transformative healing power of a single dream.

Beebe then outlines three "paradoxical conditions which the Jungian analytic tradition has set up for understanding and working with the dream." Paradox one honors the fact that "the dream is alive, yet operates to bring an old attitude to its 'death.'" As Beebe states, "That the dream is alive is of course at the heart of Jung's approach to the psyche. His notion of the living reality of the inner environment, the psyche, implies that the dream needs to be approached, like Yosemite, with an attitude of respect, with an ecological mindedness. We should backpack the dream, not strip mine it. We should be careful how we develop it. We can pollute it." According to Beebe, "the second paradox of Jungian dream work concerns the therapeutic relationship in which the dream, and the work on the dream, happen." The dream registers the therapeutic relationship, as a "picture of an objective, unconsciously structured transference/countertransference which is evolving, like an alchemical experiment." Beebe characterizes the third and final paradox: "The dream depicts the actual situation in the unconscious, yet its symbolic language defends against direct insight into that situation and can be exploited by sophisticated defenses against taking its meaningful content seriously."

In the last section of the book, entitled "A Fantasia on Integrity," Beebe offers a fairy tale of "Three Army Surgeons," which concerns a lack of integrity. The tale teaches us what is involved in preserving and acting on our own integrity. In other words, taking responsibility for our actions. Beebe deduces that the three surgeons, "the would-be healers of integrity, are left with a longing for wholeness." The moral Beebe draws from the fairy tale is that "the chastened recognition of compromised integrity has produced a hunger for genuine healing."

To conclude, John Beebe has accomplished an astonishing feat of integrating the myriad elements of integrity into a whole. This book itself has integrity; it stands on its own as a sound treatise. In the very act of reading it, we find that John Dewey's words ring true: "Aesthetic experience is experience in its integrity."

DAVID H. ROSEN

College Station, Texas

Acknowledgments

I WOULD LIKE TO THANK Tom Insel for suggesting to me almost a decade ago that I might write a book on "authenticity." In the fall of 1989 the members of the third-year seminar group of the C. G. Jung Institute of San Francisco invited me to give a seminar on a topic of my choosing. I selected "Integrity in the Analytic Relationship." This largely process-oriented seminar quickly convinced me of two things that I had already sensed in my own psychotherapy office. The first was that integrity is a palpable reality in any effort at deep communication. The second was that psychology has provided almost no language with which to approach this reality. I began to long for the chance to work out some ideas on the subject. At about this time, Robert Hinshaw was arranging an opportunity for me to teach at the C. G. Jung–Institut Zurich, and I imagined my next chance to pursue the topic would be there. As it happened, an angel must have been listening, because only a few months later a Zurich analyst, Verena Kast, suggested to Carolyn Fay and David Rosen that I might like to follow her in the Fay Lecture Series.

For helping to clarify essential concepts I particularly thank: D. R. Shackleton Bailey, Edward Edinger, Robert Grudin, Joseph Henderson, James Jarrett, A. A. Long, Victor Mair, Ian

McMorran, Andrew Samuels, Robert Segal, Sonu Shamdasani, June Singer, Murray Stein, Howard Teich, Marina Warner, Herb Wiesenfeld, William Willeford, Neal Wood, Yi Wu, and Polly Young-Eisendrath. Several of my patients and consultees who must remain unnamed but contributed so much material at the heart of the theme deserve special gratitude.

For creating a forum that makes the articulation of new psychological ideas possible, I want to thank Carolyn Fay. I also appreciate the graciousness in College Station of Deborah Voorhees, Frank McMillan III, Steve Worchel, Shirley Bovey, and the audience who listened so attentively that I began to hear, myself, what I was trying to say. I am still cheered by David Rosen's belief in me and by his role in bringing this book to publication.

One person, caring that the manuscript itself would have integrity, made the articulation of these ideas secure. That is Adam Frey, who has earned a permanent debt of gratitude that it will be a pleasure to try to repay.

Integrity
in
Depth

Prologue

IN THE COURSE OF WRITING, I mentioned to one of my patients that I was working on a book. "What on?" she asked. "Integrity," I replied. "Oh," she said, "that's when you take responsibility for what you do."

Debate swirls about in many fields — architecture, politics, medicine, economics — over how people should go about taking responsibility for what they do. Out of these discussions, some interesting ideas get generated, and sometimes beautiful human behavior results. But such discourse is almost never psychological.

This book develops the topic from a psychological angle. It explores how it is possible for people to take responsibility for what they do. My intention, however, remains moral: to open a space within psychology where integrity can begin to take responsibility for what it does.

I.

A Psychological Definition of Integrity

THE WORD INTEGRITY

OF THE QUALITIES WE SEEK in ourselves and in each other, surely integrity is among the most important. One measure of our need for it may be that we rarely allow ourselves an examination of the concept itself. To do so would be to betray an unspoken philosophic, poetic, and psychological rule of our culture: not to disturb the mystery of what we desire most. Clarification would threaten integrity, a word we have used like a magic spell to protect what is purest in us from danger.

This beautiful word, integrity, can create a state of grace in the person blessed by being said to possess it. I have spent many years pondering the meaning of this elusive reality around which so much of everyone's fantasy and anxiety is organized. After years of experience in analytical psychotherapy, both as patient and as practitioner, I am convinced of integrity's central importance in human psychology, and in this book I will explore the topic in depth. Our job will be to try to understand integrity better — to risk the mystery, perhaps, by diving beyond the charm cast by the shimmering surface of the word down into the cold, unexplored waters of the archetype that hides below.

Let us start more objectively, then, with a look at the map we have been given for this largely unexplored territory. Let us examine the word integrity itself. Every culture seems to have some word for "uprightness" and the inner sense of "standing tall" which that body image conveys,[1] but *integrity* is a much more abstract and less embodied term. It means, literally, the state of being untouched. *Tag*, its Sanskrit root, as the game we still call by this name implies, means to touch or handle. Out of this root come words like tact, taste, tax, and contaminate. *Integ* means *not* touched or handled. Small wonder so few people have handled this topic!

The Latin adjective *integer* was a way of complimenting the well-known probity of the classical Roman character. *Integer* meant intact, whole, complete, perfect, honest, and from it derives the English adjective entire, as well as the mathematical name integers that we accord to the individual "whole" numbers, like one, two, and three, each of which stands for a quality and a quantity unique to itself. *Integritas,* the abstraction made from integer, began to enter the Latin language during the lifetime of Cicero, and present-day Latin dictionaries accord him the distinction of being the first to use it, as he is also the first to have used *qualitas* and *quantitas.* Perhaps he even coined the term; he was fond of supplying abstract endings that gave to the sometimes rigid Latin language the conceptual flexibility of Greek. (*Moralis* and *imago,* the sources of our "moral" and "image" are other words whose use seems to originate with him, along with the one that best defines his overall intention, *humanitas.*)[2]

By Cicero's time, the waning years of the Roman Republic, *integritas* had become an abstraction in a more psychological sense: it had become something experience-distant, and the use of this word in his writings is frequently edged with irony and sadness. He sometimes uses it to provoke guilt, with a hortatory nostalgia for a better Rome. One of his earliest recorded uses of the word was in 70 B.C. in his prosecution of the recent governor of Sicily, Gaius Verres, on behalf of the Sicilian people, from whom Verres had bled the equivalent of close to a million dollars in today's money. Cicero wanted the senatorial court in Rome to hear what was at stake:

> For indeed, in these days, no surer means of securing our country's welfare can be devised than the assurance of the Roman people that—given the careful challenging of judges by the prosecutor—our allies, our laws, our country can be safely guarded by a court composed of senators; nor can a greater disaster come upon us all than a conviction, on the part of the Roman people, that the Senatorial Order has cast aside all respect for truth and integrity, for honesty and duty [". . . neque tanta fortunis omnium pernicies potest accedere quam opinione populi Romani rationem veritatis, integritatis, fidei, religionis ab hoc ordine abiudicari"]. And I feel in consequence that I have undertaken to rescue an important part of our body politic, a part that is sick unto death and almost beyond recovery. . . .[3]

The nostalgia that accompanies this early, Ciceronian use of the word is one of the shades of meaning accompanying its use today; from its inception it has been an old-fashioned value, in danger of being eclipsed or lost, in need of defense or restoration. Integrity is a word used to defend threatened pride. In August of 1990, George Bush used the word twice in a single week. The first time was to assure the American people that he stood by the integrity of his son Neil Bush, who was being accused of improper dealings in the savings and loan scandal. The second time was to announce his determination to defend the integrity of Kuwait.

Yet far from being a value reserved for the old and established, defending their turf, integrity is often a burning issue for the person who is seeking to fashion a reputation. Cicero was thirty-six years old when he published the Verrine Orations;[4] he meant them to enhance the reputation he would need, as a newcomer to Rome's aristocratic circles of power, to become a consul of Rome. His mention of integrity is ironically a symptom of his ambition.

Benjamin Franklin, who came to Philadelphia as a young man to escape an endless apprenticeship in his father's Boston, worked out for himself in the early years in his new city "a scheme to attain moral perfection by an art of Virtue."[5] This involved him in keeping a list of Virtues: Temperance, Silence, Order, Resolution, Frugality, Industry, Sincerity, Justice, Moderation, Cleanliness, Tranquility, and Chastity. As Franklin tells us: "I made a little Book in which I allotted a Page for each of the Virtues. I rul'd each Page with red Ink so as to have seven Columns, one for each Day of the Week, marking each Column with a Letter for the Day. I cross'd these Columns with thirteen red Lines, marking the Beginning of each Line with the first Letter of one of the Virtues, on which Line & in its proper Column I might mark by a little black Spot every Fault I found upon Examination, to have been committed respecting that Virtue upon that Day." Franklin even had the idea of publishing a book to be called "The Art of Virtue," which would "have endeavoured to convince young Persons, that no Qualities were so likely to make a poor Man's Fortune as those of Probity & Integrity."[6]

Fortunately, Franklin had the sense to recognize almost immediately that he was in danger of offending his likely audience by his pride, and so he added Humility to his original list of twelve virtues, making a baker's dozen, and never wrote his Art of Virtue. Of his effort to achieve humility, Franklin observes drily, "I cannot boast of much Success in acquiring the *Reality* of this Virtue; but I had a good deal with regard to the *Appearance* of it." He tells us:

I made it a Rule to forbear all direct Contradiction to
the Sentiments of others, and all positive Assertion of my
own. I even forbid myself . . . the Use of every Word or
Expression in the Language that imported a fix'd Opinion;
such as *certainly, undoubtedly,* &c. and I adopted instead of
them, *I conceive, I apprehend,* or *I imagine* a thing to be so
or so, or so it appears to me at present.—When another asserted something that I thought an Error, I deny'd my self
the Pleasure of contradicting him abruptly, and of showing
immediately some Absurdity in his Proposition; and in an-
swering I began by observing that in certain Cases or Circumstances his Opinion would be right, but that in the present case there *appear'd* or *seem'd* to me some Difference, &c.

The interesting thing is that in giving up the insistence on
his integrity, the young Franklin did begin to take on more
of the reality of this quality, a fact perceived by others, so that
his underlying project of self-promotion was able to succeed
on the basis of his transformed character:

I soon found the Advantage of this Change in my Manners.
The Conversations I engag'd in went on more pleasantly. The
modest way in which I propos'd my Opinions, procur'd them
a readier Reception and less Contradiction; I had less Mortification when I was found to be in the wrong, and I more
easily prevail'd with others to give up their Mistakes & join
with me when I happen'd to be in the right. And this Mode,
which I at first put on, with some violence to natural Inclination, became at length so easy & so habitual to me, that
perhaps for these Fifty Years past no one has ever heard a
dogmatical Expression escape me. And to this Habit (after
my Character of Integrity) I think it principally owing, that
I had early so much Weight with my Fellow Citizens, when
I proposed new Institutions, or Alterations in the old; and so
much influence in public Councils when I became a Member.

Franklin concludes with a display of his mastery of this strategy of modesty: "For I was but a bad Speaker, never eloquent, subject to much Hesitation in my choice of Words, hardly correct in Language, and yet I generally carried my Points."[7]

This is the synthesis of integrity and self-promotion that was for Franklin the way to reputation and success. So also had it been for Cicero, a "new man" to the Roman oligarchy that held power in the late Republic,[8] using his gift of eloquence to win what no Roman had for thirty years: the consulship when his father had not been consul before him. Franklin, also a "new man" to colonial Philadelphia, likewise achieved an honored place in the circle of those forming the new national government by downplaying his considerable gift for argument. Both make integrity—specifically that word—central not just to their personal ethics, but to their program for self-advancement.

Both Cicero and Franklin ended up writing books late in life that have become manuals for the young person who might also wish to succeed—Cicero's *De Officiis*, to which we shall return, and Franklin's *Autobiography*, of which we have already tasted. These books have had incalculable influence on our conception of integrity. In concluding that integrity is central to success in life, both Cicero and Franklin discover a paradox: integrity, which would seem to presuppose a conscience uncontaminated by concern for political advantage, cannot be separated from personal ambition for approval. Rather, it is the right way to win that approval. Integrity involves our dealings with others, and ambition to win their respect is part of its archetypal constellation; integrity is a self-consistency that is effective interpersonally. Neither Cicero's pride in his own integrity, which ultimately destroyed his political career,[9] nor Franklin's knowing struggle with a similar pride, which enabled him to achieve a lasting success, really resolve the paradox at the heart of both men's use of integrity to advance ambition. Their example threatens to drown any modern seeker of integrity, quite like Narcissus, in fascination with the possibilities of his own image.

Robert Grudin, in his book *Time and the Art of Living,* offers reflections about integrity that attempt to soften this paradox. He points to a therapeutic effect in the way time is altered for those who discover the fact of integrity:

> Integrity is usually seen as imperviousness to fear, desire and other like emotions. But we may see it with equal accuracy as superiority to present time and to the complex of emotions whose only real existence is in the present. For all the psychological and physiological conditions which test integrity —fear, desire, hunger, fatigue, disaffection, anger, pain—have little reality in memory or anticipation but rather exist for the most part in the narrow immediacy of the present. The person of integrity is a continuous person, for whom the present is a point on a line drawn out of memory and into the willed future, rather than an unpredicted and unwieldy configuration which seems to operate under its own laws. The person of integrity is no superman; he will be, from time to time, defeated, frustrated, embarrassed and completely surprised. But neither is he the common and regular dupe of circumstance, compelled (like some tourist with a pocket dictionary) to consult conscience and emotion at each new turn of events.[10]

The relationship to eternity that integrity permits puts worldly success in perspective. We might also deduce from these remarks that anyone who aspires to integrity has somehow been wounded by time, has somehow failed by wanting too much to succeed in a particular moment. The person who becomes particularly concerned with integrity is more like Cicero— writing his classic book on moral duties for his son when he sensed there was only a slim hope that the ideal of Republic would prevail—than like Franklin, eighteen centuries later, reflecting with satisfaction over the resurgence of Cicero's dream on the American continent.[11]

Cicero's book, *De Officiis*, which might be better translated *On Obligations*, is most often known to English readers as *On Duties*. It is cast as a reworking of a previous book of Stoic ethics, but it is really an etiquette of aristocratic morality written for Cicero's twenty-one-year-old son, who was studying philosophy in Athens. The importance of this book to our present purpose is that it is the leading text through which our culture has received its conception of integrity. It is the book in the background of Castiglione's *Book of the Courtier,* Rousseau's *Confessions,* and Franklin's *Autobiography.*

The theme of *De Officiis* is integrity—as a moral obligation, as a standard of reputation, and as a way of making it in the world. As Cicero's most popular modern translator, Michael Grant, has observed, it "has perhaps exercised more influence on the thought and standards of the western world than any other secular work ever written."[12] Cicero's most thorough modern commentator, Neal Wood, echoing this sentiment, tells us that *De Officiis* was "read throughout the Middle Ages and was possibly the first book of classical antiquity to come from a printing press. From the sixteenth to the nineteenth century it was staple fare for young European pupils, a universally accepted manual for gentlemanly conduct."[13]

The tone of the advice, which is cast in the form of a long letter, comes across in the following passage:

> In some ways winning a reputation is like making money. To take the latter pursuit, we are able to demonstrate the methods not only of acquiring money but also of investing it so as to provide an income which will meet our recurrent expenses and supply the necessities and amenities of life. The same applies to a reputation; first you must acquire it, and then you have to invest what you have acquired. As to the

process of acquisition, Socrates was perfectly right when he declared that there is a direct short-cut to winning a reputation: "Make yourself the sort of man you want people to think you are." (Xenophon, *Memorabilia*, II, 6, 39) For to suppose that any permanent reputation can be won by pretence, or empty display, or hypocritical talk, or by putting on an insincere facial expression, would be a serious misapprehension. . . .

Although the essence of the situation, as Socrates indicated, is that we really should *be* what we want our fellow human beings to think we are, there are certain methods of ensuring that people do in fact discover what we are like, and I will now suggest what these methods are.[14]

This sounds, at first hearing, like lectures we still get from our own fathers, and we respond with an uneasy sense that the advice *is* urging a sort of hypocrisy, or at least a moral opportunism. In *De Officiis*, Cicero traces his ethical steps from Stoic philosophy.[15] Cicero tells his son that "the Stoics' ideal is *to live consistently with nature.*"[16]

You must also understand that nature has clothed us, as it were, with two characters. One of them is universal, deriving from the fact that we all participate in the intelligence and superiority by which we surpass other animals. This intelligence is the origin of all morality and decorum, and it supplies the means to discover duty in a rational way. The other is the character bestowed separately on each individual.[17]

His word *integritas* points, I think, to the part of us that is general Intelligence, always seeking to live in accord with Nature's law. This part of our own nature is actively interested in maintaining a continuity of Nature's intent. Cicero has such confidence in this part of us that he writes, "We must of course refrain from doing anything against nature; but having taken this into consideration, let us follow our own nature; and even if we should find something better elsewhere, let us use our own nature as the standard for regulating our wills."[18]

It is possible that this conception derives from the Stoic philosopher Panaetius, who lived two generations before Cicero and whose own treatise *On Duties* was the model for the first two books of Cicero's *De Officiis*.[19] But to see the originality of Cicero's synthesis of Middle Stoic thought, we have only to compare Seneca's ideas on ethics from a few decades later, which still follow the traditional Stoic line in denying our right to trust instinctive human nature:

> Now I return to the question you want discussed, how we arrive at the first conception of the good and of rectitude. Nature could not have taught us this; it has not given us knowledge but seeds of knowledge. Some people claim that we light upon the conception by chance. But it is beyond belief that anyone has encountered the form of virtue in this way. Our school takes the view that it is observation and mutual comparison of repeated actions which has assembled this conception. In the judgment of our philosophers rectitude and the good are perceived through analogy. . . . We were familiar with bodily health. From this we have worked out that there also exists a health of the mind. Certain acts of generosity or humanity or courage had amazed us. We began to admire them as though they were perfect. . . . From such deeds . . . we have derived the idea of a good of great magnitude. . . . We saw someone . . . who was kindly to his friends, forbearing to his enemies, dutiful and pious in his public and private behavior. . . . Moreover he was always the same and consistent with himself in every action, good not through policy but under the direction of a character such that he could not only act rightly but could not act without acting rightly. We perceived that in him virtue was perfected. We divided virtue into parts: the obligation of curbing desires, checking fears, foreseeing what

has to be done, dispensing what has to be given. We grasped moderation, courage, prudence, justice, and gave to each its due. From whom then did we perceive virtue? That man's orderliness revealed it to us, his seemliness, consistency, the mutual harmony of all his actions, and his great capacity to surmount everything. From this we perceived that happy life which flows on smoothly, complete in its own self-mastery.[20]

This is the *image* of integrity, but not the idea of it; everything that might bring harmony to human nature has to be learned from the occasional poignant example. Here there is no innate, natural process, available to all, as there is in Cicero, who would have his son find the moral example he needs in the honor that already accrues to him by dint of being human.

Although *De Officiis* concerns itself with the promotion of his son as a gentleman, Cicero takes special care at the end of the book to make clear that he does not intend this advice about integrity to be used in order simply to facilitate personal pleasure. Instead, Cicero seems to hint at a supraordinate dimension that cannot exist if individual aspects of *humanitas* are pursued solely for the sake of the advantages they bring: "There can be no goodness, no generosity, no courtesy, no more than there can be friendship, if these qualities are not sought out for their own sake, but are considered to be relative to pleasure or to advantageousness."[21]

This supraordinate dimension, though Cicero does not use the word here, is integrity, and integrity must be pursued as a desideratum in itself. The implication is that the real pleasure in exercising integrity in dealings with others is the discovery of integrity itself.

Philosophy has not pursued the full implications of this archetypal idea of morality because it belongs — ahead of its time — to psychology. Cicero's is a first formulation of an idea that has come finally into its own in the self psychology of our own time, the self which knows what's good for itself. Had Cicero chosen to use, at this point, the word *integritas* for what he had in mind, he would have done later philosophy a service. Instead, despite the hint in Aquinas's use of *integritas* for the essence of wholeness,[22] "moral philosophers have rarely addressed the topic of integrity directly."[23] Integrity has remained a "neglected moral idea."[24]

THE COMPASS OF PSYCHOLOGICAL UNDERSTANDING

Now, under the pressure of the psyche to examine this part of our character at a time when it is everywhere at risk, we find the idea of integrity on the doorstep of psychology. I feel that we should take it in and nourish it. Psychology should take up the concept of integrity and differentiate what present-day psychotherapy is telling us about its meaning, even though psychology is not the natural mother of this idea. If philosophy ever remembers whom it really loves, Sophia, and has at last a workable family situation, it may return to claim the child it has abandoned. In fact there are signs that philosophers are starting to make contact with the idea of integrity.[25] But until they really claim the baby back, psychologists must do the best they can with it. Like other orphans, it may repay us with renewal in our house.

Robert Grudin, in one of the few sustained attempts to examine the concept, and to affirm its importance, points out that as we find it " 'integrity' is a strangely hollow word. Of all the major ethical nouns in English, 'integrity' alone lacks a concomitant adjective, neither 'integral' nor 'integrated' adequately conveying its meaning. It is a kind of orphan noun, a word untranslatable into practical terms. Apparently, though our culture likes the idea of integrity, we have felt uncomfortable about

conferring it on people or actions as a positive characteristic."
Grudin tells us that

> Only three definitions of the word would seem able to sur-
> vive analytic scrutiny, and these meanings must be under-
> stood as complementary and interdependent. Integrity is
> 1. an inner psychological harmony, or wholeness;
> 2. a conformity of personal expression with psychological real-
>   ity—of act with desire, of word with thought, of face with
>   mind, of the outer with the inner self; and
> 3. an extension of wholeness and conformity with time, through
>   thick and thin. Though integrity can be, and must be, ex-
>   pressed in individual actions, it is not fully realized except
>   in terms of continuity.
>   Thus understood, integrity may be defined as psychologi-
> cal and ethical wholeness, sustained in time. . . . Integrity
> . . . is not a painfully upheld standard so much as a prolonged
> and focused delight.[26]

Delight! This is the part of integrity Cicero could not get
across to his son.[27] Yet delight is what everyone who stumbles
upon this part of themselves eventually registers, and the pleasure we take in integrity is the natural starting point for a psychology, rather than a philosophy of integrity. Delight is after
all what integrity meant for Rousseau. As William Willeford
has recently reminded us: "In a bit of fanciful but illuminating
anthropology, Rousseau imagines savages just before they took
the first step toward the inequality that characterizes all of the
more complex societies. These people were accustomed to singing and dancing unselfconsciously in front of their huts or around
a great tree. The step toward inequality came when each of them
began to want to be admired by the others, with the result that
his sense of self-worth came to be determined by public opinion
as to who could sing and dance the best."

As Willeford perceives, "Rousseau's myth implies that there is a form of self-validation prior to the envious perversion of desire that came to inflict his singers and dancers, and that this fundamental form of self-validation has been, or could be, the basis of community of more authentic individuals than they became and than most people now are."

"Feeling is the name" Willeford gives "for the psychic process essential to this knowledge of one's individual essence and its reaching out into the world of others,"[28] and his choice of this one of Jung's four fundamental functions of consciousness as the one *primary* to the experience of our integrity is significant. Willeford clearly believes that the psychological function of feeling is fundamental both to the discovery of our integrity and to the delight we are able to take in it—Rousseau's savages, singing and dancing around a great tree.

Like Grudin, Willeford gives an eros spin to the idea of integrity, which ever since the Stoics had seemed to belong securely to the realm of logos—as a duty, as something to know about, take responsibility for, get right, watch. Willeford follows Jung in suggesting that we might better honor the self through eros/love than through logos/injunction. By entering into a loving relation to it, we delight the self, and the self's delight passes through us as a pleasure we can feel and enjoy. Willeford finds the model for this process in the mother-infant interaction, but we may find this joy expressed also in the ecstatic Christianity of John of the Cross. There John, however, is more the passive partner of an active beloved God-incarnating Self.[29]

In present-day analytical psychology, our interest is in taking the active role in relation to the self—meeting it with mirroring empathy and active interest. But, as Willeford points out, this model of self-validation need not be a self-conscious activity. Rather, the integrity of the self is something we feel, as the mother feels her baby, and as the baby feels when its experience is received by the mother. This is a relational viewpoint, a psychological perspective that accords with the experience of contemporary adults in psychotherapy and in psychological communities that honor self-discovery. When an individual's own integrity flourishes in relationship, both patient and therapist share the discovery of the integrity of interpersonal process as well. This shared field of integrity is the ground of any depth psychotherapy,[30] and it is impossible to understand the burgeoning of psychotherapy in our century if one does not recognize the profound pleasure that the discovery of integrity brings.

But our search for the psychological definition of integrity cannot be confined to the experience of its pleasure, self-validating though that pleasure is. Just as frequently (and some might argue, more frequently) integrity is located through the experience of violation. We may not even know we have a self until it becomes anxious, or angry—or until it has been raped. Kohut, Langs, and Masson have concentrated on the way the self responds when it is violated by the psychotherapist, in ways that range from the subtle to the gross, and psychotherapy has been forced to realize as the point comes home that its principal subject matter has always been, not, as Freud thought, pleasure and unpleasure but rather integrity and violation.[31]

It has also become imperative to recognize that the psyche's issue here is not just a *fantasy* of violation, fertile for exploration and best handled by a metapsychology like Freud's or an archetypal psychology like Hillman's, but, as the earlier Freud recognized and then abandoned, a literal violation that demands concrete response. If the psyche is to ground itself in a sense of its own reality and the fact of its boundaries, therapists have to do something to acknowledge when they transgress those boundaries, and to atone for the violation of them. Like the real body, the subtle body of the psyche demands respect for its limits — and all hell breaks out when they are not respected.[32] Psychotherapists feel the shockwaves of such disruptions in their own bodies. My head or my stomach can wrench when a patient breaks an appointment, or suddenly alters the frame of our work by the wrong kind of extra call. If I break my own agreements, I will see evidence of post-traumatic reactions in the patient's material, and I have no doubt that these are also bodily felt by the patient. The bodily sensations and the associations point to the reality of inner psychic boundaries, which require respectful handling. They are signals of outrage, another indication that there is a pre-existing integrity.

Patients expect a therapist to uphold integrity in the analytic relationship. The therapist is supposed to stand for something. It may be just as hard on a patient to witness a lapse of integrity by the therapist as to be violated by the therapist in other ways. Years ago I tried to formulate a basic code of ethics for myself, to guide my clinical practice and my supervision of other psychotherapists. I decided that a psychotherapist has two basic obligations. The first is to protect the self-esteem of the client at all costs, even when the client is actively provoking the therapist to injure that self-esteem. The second is to protect the setting or institution of psychotherapy itself as a place where healing can occur. (Notice that neither of these responsibilities requires the therapist to cure the patient.) This would mean, for instance, that a therapist may terminate a psychotherapy that is at impasse or has become destructive, but in doing so, rather than blaming the patient, the therapist will make it clear that what has transpired demonstrates only the therapist's present limits, leaving open the possibility that the patient may be able to work effectively with another therapist whose skill and holding capacity are greater or different.

Psychotherapy, as Jung ever insisted, is a dialectical procedure, and it is not hard to find Hegel in the dialectic of integrity. If pleasure is the thesis, and violation the antithesis of the psychological experience of integrity, recovery is the synthesis. We have perhaps learned most about the psychology of integrity from people who are in recovery, including, importantly, people in the Alcoholics Anonymous–derived Twelve Step programs, of whom at present John Bradshaw is the most eloquent spokesperson.[33] I have seen many people in recovery from former psychotherapies, who need to tell themselves and someone else the tale of how that therapy did wrong by them. Some end by being grateful to the injury for sharpening their sense of who they are. Within an ongoing psychotherapy, the hours in which I have learned most about integrity have come when patients have brought me their rage at something I have unconsciously done, and I have found it in myself to see exactly what they were talking about and why it was a violation. Sometimes these unconscious aggressive actions were my way of retaliating for injuries I had earlier felt at their hands, and they could now acknowledge them. The respect for each other and for the self that can follow upon such moments of recovery is extraordinary. It can be achieved only in exchanges of mutual honesty and care, where what is disclosed and counterdisclosed itself respects the boundaries of the relationship.

This dialectic of integrity as we discover it in psychotherapy does not occur only through the feeling function, although Willeford is surely right in giving feeling the preeminent role in sorting out the intense affects invariably involved and in setting up the relationships in which these affects can be played out. In our century, Jung is the theorist who has given the most thought to what the true basis of a psychological consciousness might be. His reading of literature, psychiatry, religion, and philosophy convinced him that a minimum of four basic approaches were needed, like the direction points on a compass, to provide a complete psychological survey of any subject. If we want to understand integrity psychologically, we should take Jung's model seriously as our major available instrument.

In his book *Psychological Types,* he calls his compass points thinking, intuition, sensation, and feeling. These he describes as the "functions of consciousness," the minimum elements of a complete psychology.[34] In the subtitle of the first English translation of the book, he calls this approach "the psychology of individuation," meaning that he believes he has supplied the pattern for the differentiation of consciousness in the person who is becoming psychologically self-aware. I have spent many years pursuing the implications of this theory, and I am sure Jung means that a psychologically developed individual will have a differentiated self-knowledge that includes all four kinds of intelligence — a feeling, a thinking, an intuitive, and a sensation awareness.

This is a point of view from which I have drawn much sustenance, and I believe it can nourish integrity's consciousness of itself as well. So far we have approached integrity through two of these functions. We started with the thinking function, exemplified by Cicero's naming of integrity as an abstraction, and concluded that philosophy has rarely explored the logical implications of this significant name. We turned for help to psychological writers who have handled integrity in terms of the feeling function. We discovered a dialectic within that feeling function: a thesis of delight, an antithesis of violation, and a synthesis of recovery. I then set up another dialectic between feeling and thinking in opposing experience and its interpretation. Throughout, I have mirrored what I have found in the literature, and I hope at least some have chafed, as I have, at the rational tidiness of this approach to the psychology of integrity.

Willeford is right in his happy definition of integrity as "being true to oneself in abundance and limitation,"[35] but it would restrict us too much to follow him in using a feeling evaluation, even in dialectic with thinking as good as his, to encompass our experience of integrity. In fact, feeling is ill-equipped to confront either the abundance or the limitation of integrity, since these are irrational givens beyond the province of feeling to control.

Like thinking, feeling is a function Jung places on the rational axis of his compass of personality,[36] the axis of our psychological consciousness that is interested in ordering experience through understanding. This recognition that feeling-understanding is as rational in its aim and design as thinking-understanding was a landmark in the history of thought, a break with tradition, because philosophy had always confused feeling with emotion, denying it the status of reason and mistaking it, in a misapplied compliment to the feeling function, for the affective influence of the irrational. Thus Pascal's "The heart has its reasons which reason knows nothing of."[37] But Jung saw through the pretensions of the feeling-types to recognize, as a good psychologist, that feeling can deny or attempt to control the irrational just as effectively as thinking. In fact, feeling loves to bring order to emotion (as we see in the rhetoric of psychotherapy: sort it out, work it through, talk it out), and the means it employs in so doing are rational, involving the conscientious application of values and relationship. And feeling is involved, just as much as thinking, in "judging" which feelings go where, and how much weight is to be put on them. Feeling is an option we can exercise in judging our experience of integrity.[38] It is a way of making that experience more harmonious to ourselves and, if we want it to be that way, more in harmony with a universal order of duty or of love.

Integrity, however, is given to us in particular, not ideal, circumstances. The reassuring, transcendental idea of integrity as human dignity has to contend with the reality the existentialists have noticed, that we are just "thrown" here, into the families and cultures we get and the compromises of integrity they very early demand from us. One way to understand the perennial popularity of the Faust myth is that, in our early childhoods, we have all sold out.[39] How can psychology deal with this just so-so-ness, this unevenness in our integrity— integrity as we find it, not as it ought to be?

To get at the reality of integrity, we need to use functions of the given, not functions of option—what Jung calls the irrational functions and the Myers Briggs Type Indicator calls the "perceiving" functions: sensation and intuition. Through them we can get a factual read-out on the status of our integrity and a vision of its potential for development. This is what happens when, following Jung, we allow our psychotherapy to include dreams and conscientiously attempt to understand what the dreams are saying. Unfortunately, most psychotherapists have tried to handle dreams through thinking and feeling, the rational functions, with mediocre results, which perhaps is why so few therapists continue to bother with them. This is too bad, for if they approached the dream in the right psychological way, its yield to them and their patients would be enormous. What is this way, and how may it illuminate the psychological definition of integrity? Joseph Henderson has given the best statement of it I know in an extraordinary passage from a little-known paper. I would like to quote extensively from it here:

> A true interpretation is only made possible by mobilizing certain psychological functions of perception whereby the dream content, together with the dreamer's associations, can be lifted from a subliminal to a manifest position. In terms of Jungian psychology there are two functions of perception, intuition and sensation. If these are outwardly directed, i.e. extraverted, they are functions for perceiving the outer world

of things and people. Intuition perceives the variety and the possibilities for developing and exploiting these things, whereas sensation perceives the specific identity of each person or thing in relation to each other person or thing in present time. If these functions are directed inwardly, i.e. introverted, they perceive the activity of the psyche in much the same way. Introverted intuition perceives the variety and the possibility for development of the inner images, whereas introverted sensation perceives the specific image which defines the psychic activity that needs immediate attention.

If now we apply this kind of functioning to the perception of a dream, we meet both of these functions in a state of collision, and this is one reason why attempts at dream interpretation are frequently so difficult and their results so unsatisfactory. The intuitive function sees many things the dream might mean and is highly productive in summoning forth a wide variety of free associations, especially of the kind Jung has called amplifications, and he encourages the interpreter of dreams to look for as many of these as time and the capacity for doing it may allow. But no amount of amplifications can give the true meaning of a dream. This must come from introverted sensation which can single out from all the possible meanings that one meaning which tells us what is the specific psychic activity behind the dream and how it can be brought into the foreground of consciousness.

In this process many beautiful jewels which intuition gathers to make a glittering necklace of interpretations may have to be sacrificed and the one interpretation of the dream that survives is like a humble, rough field stone. Yet this single stone may become more important symbolically than all the others put together. Having said this, the intuitive function, however, may argue that no interpretation of a dream is ever final and that the one interpretation which seemed so immutable looks different at different times and in different lights. There is no absolutely final interpretation to a dream and I often find it easier to see what a dream means by reading it over days, weeks or months later. Its meaning has a way of changing in the light of fresh insights and new experiences. Therefore, intuition and sensation seem to set up a kind of functional dialectic which does justice to the mysterious nature of the psyche.[40]

When this dialectic of dream interpretation is brought to bear on the problem of integrity, it yields immediate and dramatic results, opening up even the most demonic aspects of ourselves to moral scrutiny. For example, even the strongest erotic compulsions can be seen in the light of their effect upon integrity.

A homosexual man, caught up in a crush on an unresponsive new friend, dreamed that he was watching Rita Hayworth near the end of her life, at the time when she had Alzheimer's and was cared for round the clock. Moving on a new, somewhat seductive nurse who had come on the scene, Rita tried to pull this young woman toward her, yelling, "Make love! Make love! Make love!"

The dreamer's intuition was already too strong where the possibilities of relationship were concerned. He had no trouble seeing that this dream referred to his new friendship. The dream, however, brought to light several elements of the current reality that had been overlooked by the dreamer's sensation function. He was forced to recognize the out-of-control Love Goddess as an image of his own eagerness for relationship, as well as to see that his friend was being, like the new nurse, unconsciously seductive. This recognition supported a greater realism in his approach to the relationship; he backed off, protecting both his own integrity and that of his new friend. They were able later to get into a more boundaried long-term relationship.

I know of no more powerful technique for the regular perception of the specifics of integrity than careful attention to dreams, for it is in dreams that we experience our limits and the limits of others as implications of our own attitudes. By recognizing these limits, interpretation restores inner boundaries and gives us the will to rectify the instability of a particular situation. For the most part, as Henderson points out, we need the function of sensation to make us realize that we see in our dreams not just ideas or possibilities, or images of our feelings, but facts, which have to be registered and acted upon.

This reality confronts us with our limitations, but we also need a psychological function to understand this part of integrity in relation to a wider whole. The function that does the job of giving us the bigger picture is intuition. Intuition brings us a sense of the ecology of integrity, for intuition is the function that gives a feeling for the entire pattern operating in a given moment. The Rita Hayworth dream put an archetypal image of love-readiness in context, and the dreamer, associating this image to aspects of his mother complex, got insight into the limited capacity for his passion to display integrity at this time. The mother archetype's judgment could not be trusted and in fact was threatening the anima that could support a more stable unfolding of his love for his friend.

Jung's theory of archetypes[41] has made it easy for us to recognize Aphrodite, and the Mother Goddess, in a dream where Rita Hayworth appears, but our psychology has yet to assimilate Jung's insight that archetypes make sense only as parts of a larger whole. By themselves, archetypes have little integrity (or only the trivial integrity that does not go beyond consistency with one's own perspective), and they are for that reason usually dangerous guides when we are trying to decide how to behave.

For Jung, the way to get past the narrowness of any single archetypal perspective was to recognize that it participated in the wider whole that he called the Self. Jung's chief model for this insight came from the Chinese philosophical conception of *Tao* (pronounced DOW). In *Psychological Types* he writes: "The meanings of *tao* are as follows: way, method, principle, natural force or life force, the regulated processes of nature, the idea of the world, the prime cause of all phenomena, the right, the good, the moral order."[42]

The Tao is a flow of life that does not stop for particular constellations. Rather it moves through them. The archetypes were not ends in themselves but means of entering the stream of Tao. For Jung, the Tao was the ground of integrity. So long as the archetypes were put into perspective by careful enough analysis of the psyche that experienced them, integrity would result. If not, inflations would threaten. Jung warned: "It is therefore of the utmost importance in practical treatment to keep the integrity of the personality constantly in mind. For, if the collective psyche is taken to be the personal possession of the individual, it will result in a distortion or an overloading of the personality which is very difficult to deal with."[43]

For this reason, Jung encouraged his patients, as he encouraged Western civilization, to a wider sense of the whole range of archetypal perspectives, so that we can see how any attitude is but one of many, with a history and a fate of its own. And he urged reliance upon the unconscious itself as the compensating principle or self-regulating system, that could even provide dreams on both sides of a question until consciousness was forced to locate its position in response to these paradoxical promptings of the Self. He also made sure the most practical translation of the *I Ching* would be made available in English to the West; so that individuals could see their choices in terms of the wider perspective of the Tao.

If we go back to the *Tao Te Ching* (written down during the second half of the third century B.C. — that is, about the same time as the early Stoic philosophers), where the idea of Tao is first formulated, we have to be struck by the fact that

Jung has emphasized Tao at the expense of its other philosophic term. This term is *te* (pronounced DUH), which has traditionally been translated as "Virtue." Since the word *Ching* means book, we might translate the *Tao Te Ching* as the Classic Book of Virtue in relation to Tao. Unfortunately, the concept of virtue has located the *te* in the *Tao Te Ching* too much in the tradition of Confucian thought, dulling the psychological force of the *te* concept. Archie J. Bahm, some years ago, tried to revitalize this book for us by interpreting Tao as "Nature" and Te as "Intelligence," so that he could translate the beginning of chapter 21 as "Intelligence consists in acting according to Nature,"[44] which brings us full circle to the Stoic conception of integrity.

Recently, a new translation of the *Tao Te Ching* by Victor Mair has translated *te* as integrity. Mair, a conscientious and respected sinologist, who knew that he was bucking Confucian tradition to find the original Taoist meaning of this concept, describes his path to this translation:

> I spent two full months trying to arrive at a satisfactory translation of *te*. Walking through the woods, riding on the train, buying groceries, chopping wood — the elusive notion of *te* was always on my mind. The final choice of "integrity" is based on a thorough etymological study of the word, together with a careful consideration of each of its forty-four occurrences in the text. In certain instances perhaps another word such as "self," "character," "personality," "virtue," "charisma" or "power" might have been more befitting. But "integrity" is the only word that seemed plausible throughout. By "integrity," I mean the totality of an individual including his or her moral stance, whether good or bad.

Mair adds that "the archaic forms of the Chinese character for *te* used in the [Ma-wang-tui] manuscripts caused me to realize that this term signified the holistic inner quality or character of a person. The basic components of the Chinese graph at the time of the writing of the *Tao Te Ching* were an eye looking straight ahead, and the heart, and a sign for movement or behavior."[45]

Te is the integrity we bring to our participation in Tao. It is traditional in Jungian thought to emphasize Tao as the way for westerners to heal themselves. I would urge a greater attention to *te*. *Te* is the part of the personality that enacts the relationship to Tao. Mair tells us: "As it is used in the *Tao Te Ching*, *te* signifies the personal qualities or strengths of the individual, one's personhood. *Te* is determined by the sum total of one's actions, good and bad. Therefore it is possible to speak of 'cultivating one's *te*.' Like karma, *te* is the moral weight of a person, which may be either positive or negative. In short, *te* is what you are."[46]

Te is not invariably in good shape; Mair points out that in the very first chapter of the Ma-wang-tui manuscripts we encounter the term *hsia-te,* which means "inferior *te*" and that "another common expression is *hsiung-te,* which signifies 'malevolent *te.*'" When *te* is cultivated, however, we experience it as an openness to connections, a recognition that "'*te* is the embodiment of the Way and is the character of all entities in the universe,' and that 'Each creature, each object has a *te* which is its own manifestation of the Tao.'"[47] A cultivated *te* is like an objective resonance to the Stoic conception of *sympatheia,* the hidden sympathy of all things: *te* is the compassion we display toward each other in times of crisis, and also the capacity to experience the pattern in chance events.

Appreciation of synchronicity (the meaning that can be revealed by a chance event) involves sensation in a dialectic with intuition, as in dream interpretation, but this time the manifold reality of the outer event is tied to a single intuitive meaning. An openness to such dialectic is of course the basis for using the Chinese oracle book, *I Ching.* But as Hellmut Wilhelm points out, we still have trouble getting past our rational objections to the chance procedures that are used to obtain access to the wisdom of this book:

> How is it possible that numbers and numerical formulas arrived at by a throwing of coins or a manipulation of yarrow stalks should disclose a relation that establishes a man's own fate in time and accounts for its development? That a toss of the coins or a division of a bundle of yarrow stalks should achieve such a result seems to us to relegate the oracle to the realm of coincidence. For us in the West it is hard to see how a genuine synchronicity could be arrived at by so seemingly mechanical a means.

He cites the solution of the seventeenth-century Confucian scholar Wang Fu-chih to this problem, which in Wilhelm's translation seems to assimilate the Confucian ideal of sincerity to the idea of integrity that we have already met in the Taoist conception *te:*

> Obviously Wang Fu-chih was also aware of the rational difficulty back of this doubt. For him number and numerical formulas were tools, and the manner in which they were obtained was method. Of course this method, if incorrectly applied, is just as likely to obscure the law as to reveal it. Something more is needed to put one in a position to make proper use of the tools and the method. It is not something that can be rationally induced at will; it is an attitude, through which the tools and the method can be brought to bear effectively. Indeed, modern psychology also has noted the existence of a particular attitude through which synchronicity can be apprehended; there must be an openness to such connections. Unlike the psychologists, however, Wang Fu-chih designated the requisite attitude "integrity." "Only a man

of the highest integrity," he says, "can understand this law; basing himself on its revelation he can grasp the symbols, and observing its small expressions he can understand the auguries."[48]

With the entry, through Jung's espousal of the *I Ching*, of this extreme of Chinese thought into our present-day psychological attitude, we close the circle that bounds integrity as a topic for psychology. Cicero, drawing upon Stoic philosophy, could postulate an innate ethicality by means of which it is possible to discriminate our obligations to live in accord with universal Law. Wang Fu-chih could assert a developed Confucian sincerity that is open to all the connections implied by Tao. These are psychological definitions of integrity taken to their limits. Through them, integrity becomes a psychological experience — less an austere static wholeness than a dynamic participation in the needs of the whole. Integrity implies an ecological sense of the harmony and interdependence of all the parts of the whole, a felt sense of the entirety of any situation.[49]

This ecological consciousness provides integrity with its moral power in relating inner self to outer contingency. It also unites apparent opposites in prior world philosophy and religion. The Western conception of integrity emerges out of a philosophical dialectic between the thinking and feeling functions that has been fostered in our own time through the practice of psychotherapy; the Eastern conception of integrity is a traditional spiritual attitude based on a dialectic between the sensation and intuitive functions in the practical interpretation of experience. Both conceptions of integrity presuppose a connection with ourselves that permits an ethical connection to everything else in the universe.

2.

The Shadow and Integrity

THE SIGNAL

UNTIL IT IS IN DANGER of being compromised, we scarcely recognize integrity as a fact of our nature. A proper starting point
for the discovery of integrity, then, is the experience of anxiety.
We are contemplating a course of action, have gone so far as
to invest in a certain way of proceeding, and find a strange, nag-
ging unease somewhere at the core of our will. Upon the most
meticulous self-examination, we conclude that the course we
have embarked upon is not founded, after all, on the motive
we had supposed. We stop to examine the real motive. However unattractive the ground we uncover through this inquiry,
finding the truth brings relief. Only then do we feel secure in
figuring out what we must do.

Jung called this process facing and integrating the shadow.
It has become such an everyday part of decision making in many
of our lives that I have chosen to describe it in the first person
plural, as "our" common experience. I know for myself that I
watch this insecurity do its work in nearly every hour of my
psychotherapy practice, and a similar anxiety hovers over the
"interventions" I choose to make in responding to my patients.

Only recently have I begun to realize that this experiencing
and examining of anxiety is an ethical process in which, as the
French philosopher Emmanuel Levinas says, "one's infinite obli-

gation to the other" is expressed.[1] What this *other* may be is problematic: it might be either another person or a value associated with the self, in fact it is almost always both. It can be felt as an objective fact of one's own being or truly as an otherness belonging to someone or something else. It is the function of integrity to remember our obligation to this other, and anxiety reminds us that we have an obligation to the obligation. It pulls at us like a center that will not hold or like a marriage we must make work.

Just now, when I began to examine this central anxiety, I left undefined the questioned course of action, the motive, how the action finally decided upon differed from the one originally contemplated, and who might have a stake in the outcome. Filling in these blanks is the usual territory of moral philosophy, in its discussion of conflicting obligations and responsibilities. My hope is that in reading this you have supplied a situation from your own experience that allows you to wonder whether you have acted with integrity and that enables you to feel your anxiety as a function of your integrity. I notice that as I approach our topic in this fashion, letting you do the work, I begin to question myself. All examples are revealing of the person who puts them forward. Am I keeping specifics back for reasons of my own? Am I really being fair to you not to give a fleshed-out example? Is this safe approach keeping a deeper reality from speaking within me; am I hiding in the unconnected, logical regions of the mind?

Psychotherapy has taught us to ask ourselves these questions. The dialectic of integrity depends, as Socrates knew, upon an endless self-questioning, driven by an uneasiness at the core of the questioner. In the language of psychoanalysis, this uneasiness is both signal anxiety, telling us the self is in danger, and separation anxiety, indicating that a vital relationship is at risk. It is the sign of an unconscious perception of separation from the self. Pursuing this uneasiness is the most frequent way that we stumble upon the fact that there is something there to lose.

With the discovery of the scope of the shadow, not just by the twentieth century's psychotherapy, but also by its history, our questioning of ourselves has taken on a dimension of depth and urgency, so that not only the nature but also the priority of moral inquiry has been altered.[2] Levinas has recently told us that how "being" justifies itself, rather than what being is, has become the primary issue of philosophy. He now speaks of "ethics as first philosophy."[3]

As a student of Jung, equipped with a conceptual language that includes notions of personal shadow, archetypal shadow, and absolute evil, as well as ego, Self, and conscience, I can be lulled into thinking I understand this ethical territory better than I do.[4] Zurich-trained analysts often speak of the ethical confrontation with the unconscious as an *auseinandersetzung,* a "having it out with" each archetype as one might sit down and have a frank talk with a friend.[5] Applied to the shadow, this image of confrontation carries the connotation of courage, like someone facing down a bully. Jung was a courageous man, and this may have been his own experience, but the formula does not convey all the ways that integrity functions in the process. In my experience integrity is found not only in the courage to stand up to shadow, but in the emotions of uncertainty which force one to admit there is a problem in the first place.

The decision to approach the shadow involves anxiety, doubt, shame, and a desire to repair the relationship with an other whose needs I have somehow missed. My recognition of the need to look at shadow starts with a painfulness, a stoppage, an absence of the sense of well-being, and an agitation from within to feel okay again. Or I can be feeling too good, and suddenly realize that I am secretly afraid. I think these are symptoms of integrity, but far from representing a heroic possibility, they go by clinical names like anxiety, depression, counterphobia, and hypomania and seem to be founded on what Jung called "a justified doubt in oneself."[6] It is not easy to face a compromise with integrity, and it is arduous work to undo one (hence the appropriateness of Jung's image of the hero's task for this part of the work), but we are helped at the outset by a pressure from within that is instinctive. When we face a problem of integrity, we are caught by an archetypal drive to restore order to a troubled state.

The world has often tried to visualize the troubled "state" of a compromised integrity by means of a political image. Stories as different as *Oedipus Rex, Hamlet,* and the Watergate scandal express the drama of integrity through the image of a disordered polity. Watching *Oedipus Rex,* we feel the mounting pressure upon Oedipus to discover that the problem in Thebes is himself; in the theater with *Hamlet,* we grow impatient for the Prince to get past his scruples and take King Claudius on; and viewing the Watergate hearings on television we longed for Nixon to confess. Only then can Thebes, Denmark, or America get its integrity back.

We should not be too hasty to deliteralize these political images into intrapsychic ones. The political image is one that has been elaborated with care in many of our culture's major texts on integrity. The Taoist-Confucian *I Ching,* Plato's *Republic,* and Machiavelli's *The Prince,* for example, leave no doubt that the governance of a political entity is at issue, even though these books also invite us to apply their precepts to decisions that feel more personal.

In action, integrity does not seem to split moral decision making into realms of inner and outer governance, and neither do people who come to psychotherapy. We come to psychotherapy to learn how to take better care of self and others, but in the realm of our responsibility for them, self and others are not split. Rather, as Kohut has taught us, the self we encounter when the ego descends into its depths is embedded in a matrix of selfobjects, other people used as extensions of our personhood and as important to us therefore as we are. Our very reality as psychological beings is political, requiring the highest degree of comprehension and care from us, like a country entrusted to a leader who is also one of its citizens. For this reason, we expect integrity of ourselves, and we want our psychotherapy to foster our integrity. Whether we choose the path of inner exploration or the way of helpful counseling, psychotherapy is a moral ritual, propelled by the archetypal drive to restore order. If, as is sometimes claimed, the commonest reason people turn to psychotherapy is to get over acute demoralization, we can see from the way therapy is used, the way people stay with it, and the way they return to it, that they know they cannot restore morale if they do not restore the moral process that will enable them to survive in the political realm that is the condition of their selfhood.[7]

Experience with patients in psychotherapy teaches that in the effort to restore integrity, facing the shadow is essential. It is hard to remember that it is little more than a hundred years ago that Friedrich Nietzsche first referred to the dark side of a person in this way, pointing out that "not knowing about the smallest and most everyday things and not having a sharp eye—this is what makes the earth a 'meadow of calamity' for so many . . . one could consider that nearly all bodily and mental ills of the individual result from this shortcoming. . . ."[8]

That Nietzsche, in discussing the shadow, was referring to everyday things of the soul is made clear by Liliane Frey-Rohn, who matches this quote with another, taken from the body of writings known as Nietzsche's literary bequest: "Let us become what we have yet to: good neighbors to the things closest to us."[9] This is certainly the attitude of integrity, though it may strike us today as psychologically naive. Not always would Nietzsche assume that the human race would be ready to take on the shadow just because he had included it in his menu of moral philosophy.[10] There is a sweetness in this early passage that reminds us of Socrates. The later Nietzsche is more often opposed to Socrates, but in his initial approach to the shadow, Nietzsche shares with Socrates a presumption of the individual's fidelity to the process of self-inquiry. Just as Socrates assumed that students who had discovered what Good consists in would naturally live in a good way, Nietzsche was slow to abandon belief in a natural anxiety to work out the relationship to the shadow. Even when he concluded that alienation from traditional conceptions of morality and "the transvaluation of all values" were the necessary consequences of a serious encounter with the shadow, Nietzsche continued to presume an attitude of integrity that could survive the process of moral inquiry.[11]

I think this philosophical background affects the way we conceptualize the pressure toward health in psychotherapy. We tend to take an already functioning integrity for granted, ignoring that it is anxiety for a threatened integrity that fuels the process of psychotherapy in the first place. Not recognizing this central concern of the patient mystifies the basis of healing when it works and makes it less easy to repair when it doesn't. Particularly, we tend to gloss over the compromises of integrity in the way the therapy itself is approached, seeing them as temporary resistances that will disappear on their own or as character pathology that cannot change, rather than as indications of what is asking to be healed.

The philosophies of the East do not make this mistake, which is perhaps why so many people turn to them to educate the spirit that must accompany the soul into psychotherapy. The Confucian school of philosophy, for instance, calls the essential attitude of desire for integrity *sincerity,* and there are texts in this tradition which emphasize that we can best recognize sincerity by its trait of persistent anxiety. Hexagram 12 of the *I Ching,* "Standstill," describes a period of impasse during which integrity is having trouble prevailing in the realm. By the time of the final "lines" of this hexagram, integrity begins to have a chance of exerting influence again. Line five reads:

> Standstill is giving way.
> Good fortune for the great man.
> "What if it should fail, what if it should fail?"
> In this way he ties it to a cluster of mulberry shoots.

In his commentary to this line, Richard Wilhelm shows the purposiveness of this anxiety:

> The time undergoes a change. The right man, able to restore order, has arrived. Hence "Good fortune." But such periods of transition are the very times in which we must fear and tremble. Success is assured only through greatest caution, which asks always, "What if it should fail?" When a mulberry bush is cut down, a number of unusually strong shoots sprout from the roots. Hence the image of tying something to a cluster of mulberry shoots is used to symbolize the way of making success certain. Confucius says about this line:
> "Danger arises when a man feels secure in his position. Destruction threatens when a man seeks to preserve his worldly estate. Confusion develops when a man has put everything in order. Therefore the superior man does not forget danger in his security, nor ruin when he is well established, nor confusion when his affairs are in order. In this way he gains personal safety and is able to protect the empire."[12]

Here anxiety is an expression of sincerity, and a function of integrity: it is what secures the realm.

The reality of the shadow provides ample occasion for such anxiety. Jung once summarized the findings of depth psychology in an arresting image, when he pointed out that any of the individual complexes of our unbidden emotional life — greed, ambition, lust, resentment — can "set up a shadow government of the ego."[13] What Jung calls a shadow government of the ego, the psychoanalyst Leo Rangell has called a compromise of integrity, pointing to the superego failure involved.[14] Because of the continuous activity of the complexes, integrity cannot survive without an attitude of vigilance, and we are always, in effect, restoring our integrity from some attempt at compromise. For this reason, Confucius, like Socrates, urged that we continually question ourselves.[15]

Yet many of us find it irritating to sustain the vigil. It is hard not to resent the anxiety that is integrity's method. Who wants to heed a warning light that is always going on in the control panel of the car? It is easier to assume that the signal is wrong — a sign of immaturity, fatigue, or "mental illness." More people today label and treat integrity's signal with this quasi-medical thinking than ever before. They need perhaps to consider that the part of ourselves that worries may be the healthy part, the strength of our moral fiber. When this part suffers anxiety, the signal is not wrong, it is telling us that our integrity is somehow at risk.

For most of us in the West, the state of our integrity is a felt sense that we follow with difficulty. We are not trained in moral discernment. Our task might be easier if we had an image to go with the affect, and I wish I could easily supply one. When we look, as psychologists, for an archetypal image of integrity, it is hard to come up with something compelling.

Sometimes we think of integrity as the "still, small voice" of conscience, but even this image, if it is an image, lacks a body and a face. Freud had his own explanation for the dissociation involved, which Brenner's elementary textbook of psycho-analysis presents as follows:

> . . . the child experiences his parents' prohibitions in large part as verbal commands or scolding. The consequence of this is that the superego bears a close relationship to auditory memories and in particular to memories of the spoken word. Some intuitive perception of this fact is probably responsible for the common figure of speech which refers to the "voice of conscience." In states of psychological regression, such as dreams (Isakower, 1954) and certain types of severe mental illness (Freud, 1923) the functioning of the superego is perceived in the form of spoken words which the subject experiences as coming from a source outside himself, just as his parents' commands did when he was little.[16]

I would not reason away the absence of the person of our integrity so easily. Other aspects of parental functioning, even from very early stages of our experience, do not fail to evoke a rich archetypal representation. If a human image of conscience has been repressed, an entire way of thinking and perceiving in relation to conscience is somehow being avoided.

REDISCOVERING THE PURITAN FOREFATHER

I have come to feel that this avoided person is less a terrifying personal parent than a cultural parent, and I would dare to name him as the dreaded Puritan forefather. As Robert Neville, who precedes me in making this connection, points out:

> The dominant resources for moral reflection in modern European and American culture have been those arising from the development of Liberalism, its emancipation from conservative modes of thought, its supplanting of early competitors such as Puritanism, and its competitive relations with

its dialectical offspring, Marxism. . . . With due regard for its limitations, certain of the insights of Puritanism need to be lifted ahead of the competing perspectives of Liberalism and other alternatives: namely, its emphases on the social definition of individual identity, on participation and interaction, and on responsibility.[17]

Taking the Puritans as a historical point of reference for the full-bodied practice of integrity seems a highly arbitrary choice. Integrity, as a concept, has a long and interesting history to which we shall return, to the degree that we can sketch it out. But the Puritan movement in England, a crescendo built up to during the time of Shakespeare and reaching its apogee in the mid-seventeenth century, with a long aftermath in the American colonies, was a high water mark for the culture of integrity, one that deserves careful attention in our effort to make integrity a more central psychological concern for our own day. Yet, reclaiming even a part of the Puritan moral standpoint seems quite distasteful: the Puritan is a figure we ridicule and despise.

This disparaging attitude goes back at least as far as the late 1600s, with the restoration of the British throne after twenty years of austere Puritan rule. The reaction to those years affects the tone of Samuel Johnson's 1779 *Life of Milton,* about the greatest of all Puritan writers. Apologizing some 170 years later for Johnson's, and his own, personal antipathy toward John Milton, T. S. Eliot reminds us: "The fact is simply that the civil war of the seventeenth century, in which Milton is a symbolic figure, has never been concluded."[18]

The Puritan seriousness about individual responsibility comes through at its best in Milton's autobiographical sonnets, which present us a sort of cumulative moral record of one Puritan's life. In fact, it is only with the ascendancy of Puritanism in the seventeenth century that the artist taking moral stock of his own life becomes a literary genre.[19] Milton became an exemplary figure, with the result that "we know more about him than we know about any previous Englishman."[20] The effect of Milton's autobiographical sonnets, like that of Rembrandt's self-portraits, is to make us take our own lives more seriously. The sonnets anticipate the modern ideal of individuation, and in fact present the individuation of integrity. It is hard to realize that this achievement would probably have been impossible without the Puritan background. A recent editor of Milton has noted that "the Puritan preoccupation with inner experience and personal responsibility for salvation invests each individual life with a special shape, significance, and intensity."[21]

On the other hand, this sense of duty toward self can sound relentless, as when Milton laments, on his twenty-fourth birthday, how little he has produced or developed so far:

> How soon hath Time, the subtle thief of youth,
>   Stol'n on his wing my three and twentieth year!
>   My hasting days fly on with full career.
>   But my late spring no bud or blossom show'th.[22]

Among our contemporary fears of Puritanism is our suspicion that, with its unremitting emphasis on responsibility, it will turn the idea of individuation into a persecutory notion. I well remember the way Milton's chiding sonnet haunted my college years!

The Puritan, however, had reason to distrust the laziness of the self. To bring Christ's ideal of integrity into family, commercial, and political life would require a continuous effort. Far from being reserved to martyrs, saints, mystics, and, occasionally, heretics burned at the stake, integrity itself became a conception that belonged to everyday discourse.

Before the seventeenth century, integrity was a rarely used word, nor does it appear as a personified virtue in the art or allegory of the Middle Ages and Renaissance.[23] Its projection onto women as inhumanly high standards of virginity and chastity may be a telling sign of its lack of differentiation in the psychology of the men of these times. Integrity was associated with the Christian notion of purity, but purity is an archetype which Western culture has found hard to represent. Indeed, to many modern observers the Puritan attempt to incarnate this archetype was a mistake. The Jungian analyst Adolf Guggenbühl-Craig, for instance, believes that Puritanism "is probably a perversion, some kind of sickness of a very important archetype which we hardly ever talk about and which plays a great role in all our lives. Perhaps the saying of Jesus Christ in the Sermon of the Mount, 'blessed be the pure at heart' alludes to this archetype. Purity must be a basic archetype which, however, can even hardly be put into an image. Purity—or innocence—must be an archetypal part of our psyche which is very difficult to understand; as soon as we look at it it is not pure."[24]

I think it is still possible to find value in Puritanism, but to do so we will have to look past the cardboard figure we have made of the Puritans to the forgotten values they may hold for us. This is a task for our moral discernment, for there is plenty to despise about the Puritans. The negative effects of their effort to live by conscience, the ones we associate with the American Puritans—witch burnings, a priggish austerity, the rejection of the possibility of pleasure in this world, and an overwhelming sense of guilt—suggest patriarchal oppression at its worst. Yet the Puritans were also a caring community of individuals who took their own and their neighbors' spirituality seriously.

Certainly Milton was a man who could embrace Christian purity while retaining a classical appreciation of the human. In pursuit of an education that would properly prepare him for a poetic career, Milton, who had bristled under the university experience of his day, read for his own project the entire classical literature in Latin and Greek; the Bible and its commentaries in Hebrew and Aramaic; and the important modern writers in Spanish, German, French, and Italian, achieving through his prodigious studies an erudition to rival Goethe's and dwarf Jung's. He showed an equal steadfastness in his emotional life, which took longer to prosper. At age thirty-four he went to visit a man to whom his father had lent money and came back married to the debtor's seventeen-year-old daughter. Within a month she had returned to her parents' home and did not come back. Milton decided, with what a modern biographer has called "fantastic, reckless courage, flying in the face of received respectable opinion,"[25] to write a series of pamphlets for the right of Christians to divorce on the grounds of incompatibility, holding that we ought not "enslave the dignity of man" by fixing "straiter limits to obedience than God had set."[26]

The Miltons were not divorced. Three years later Mary Milton asked her husband to take her back, along with her whole family, who were financially ruined. Milton agreed and the marriage held together until her death seven years later. At about this time he lost what had remained of his eyesight.

One senses Milton's individuation through this arduous midlife passage. In *Paradise Lost* he created a masterpiece of archetypal psychology that gives the shadow its fullest place in English poetry,[27] and *Samson Agonistes,* his final verse drama, shows a mature blind Samson who is equal to his wily Dalila. What is most admirable in Milton is that he achieves this integration without sacrifice of the ethical ideals that guided him, despite specific doctrinal shifts, throughout his life. He can be believed when, even in the midst of blindness and near poverty, he tells his contemporaries:

> . . . I argue not against Heaven's hand or will, nor bate one jot
> Of heart or hope, but still bear up and steer
> Right onward.[28]

We have grown unaccustomed to an integrity that grounds itself in submission, but interestingly our modern usage of the word "integrity" begins, as nearly as I can determine, with Milton. It is the word his biographers most invariably use to describe him. A biographer in the eighteenth century, embarrassed by Milton's anti-royalist politics, wrote: "Whatever spots or blemishes appear upon his judgment in certain points, let the charitable eye look beyond those on his immaculate integrity."[29]

Integrity, in Christian thought, originally referred to the condition of humankind before the Fall, but in the English translations of the Bible that began to appear with the rise of Puritan influence, "integrity" was used to connote the upright person's pure-hearted inclination to follow God's will. In an ironic passage in *Paradise Lost,* Milton uses the word to undercut the proud argument Eve makes to Adam, who thinks she will be less able to withstand temptation should she be found by the Tempter "single" than with her husband laboring by her side. Says Eve:

> If this be our condition, thus to dwell
> In narrow circuit strait'n'd by a Foe,
> Subtle or violent, we not endu'd
> Single with like defense, wherever met,
> How are we happy, still in fear of harm?
> But harm precedes not sin: only our Foe
> Tempting affronts us with his foul esteem
> Of our integrity. . . .[30]

Eve does not realize yet that integrity also involves an acceptance of limits imposed by God. This will be the lesson of the Fall.

The theological conception that Milton developed goes well beyond the neo-Stoic idea of a universal moral character that participates in the intelligence of God.[31] He believed that the grace of God, which for him meant continuity of integrity, can be achieved through obedience and conscience. This belief[32] was radical in a Puritan tradition that was strongly influenced by Calvin's theory of predestination, but Milton's view of integrity eventually held sway and helped to shape the Protestant thinking that informs Jung's insistence that conscience is something separate from collective morality,[33] and that a suprapersonal Self is the final cause of individuation.

In the "great invocations" of *Paradise Lost* and *Paradise Regained,* Milton addresses the spirit of God to guide him in making his renderings truthful. A recent commentator has noted, "A spirit of humble confidence pervades all of these invocations."[34] The most famous is the prayer that opens *Paradise Lost,* where after a long preamble Milton finally beseeches a divine informer of conscience:

> . . . chiefly thou, O Spirit, that dost prefer
> Before all temples the upright heart and pure,
> Instruct me, for thou knows't; thou from the first
> Wast present, and with mighty wings outspread
> Dove-like sat'st brooding on the vast abyss
> And made it pregnant: what in me is dark
> Illumine, what is low raise and support;
> That to the highth of this great argument
> I may assert Eternal Providence,
> And justify the ways of God to men.[35]

In this final line Milton is not merely trying to reconcile us to a God who allows painful things to occur in our lives; he is already trying to do justice to a central important perception, the presence of a series of divine accesses that he succinctly calls "the ways of God to men." Yet even as he recognizes the manifold paths by which God's grace is opened to us, Milton does not gloss over the problem of evil. Both God and Man bear a share of responsibility for the estrangement which

develops between them in *Paradise Lost,* and both partake in
the opportunity that the Fall provides for their eventual reconciliation. Out of this sense of partnership comes Milton's conception of the education of integrity. Indeed, he sees the main
purpose of all education to be "to repair the ruins of our first
parents by regaining to know God aright."[36] Knowledge, including the prodigious knowledge he himself possessed, was
to give strength to the integrity by which God is accessed.[37]
As a contemporary commentator puts it, "For Milton, God was
the central fact of life," and his expressions of acceptance of
God's will were "absolutely sincere."[38]

It was in the service of God that Milton worked so hard
not only as a poet but in defense of Cromwell's secular Puritan
cause. The single-mindedness of Milton defines a conception
of integrity that our age has sought to distance. Karl Marx commented that "Milton produced *Paradise Lost* for the same reason
that a silkworm produces silk," and T. S. Eliot "attacks Milton's poetry as a 'Chinese wall', casting a baleful shadow over
later poets from Dryden to Swinburne and cutting off the ar-
terial flow of cultural vitality from the Elizabethans. . . ."[39]
The effect of this criticism is to remove Milton's achievement
—his Puritan synthesis—to the other side of the world. But
as Eliot admits, the wall against Milton is of our own making;
it is we who are defended against the seventeenth-century background.

The ascendancy of Liberalism with the Restoration, rather
like our own Reagan years, was largely a retreat from integrity.
Seeing the Puritans as perverts of the superego has the unfortunate effect of making any attempt to recover a Western episte-
mology of integrity nearly hopeless. In our own day the closest
we have come is the Twelve Step programs. Mostly, the tradition since the eighteenth century has been to approach integrity through the modes of satire and irony. Pop star "Madonna"

is the latest joke at the expense of the ideal of purity. This is the cultural shadow problem which makes integrity so hard to talk about and therefore to analyze.

Yet in modern psychotherapy, and the culture which surrounds it, we have seen a surprising resurgence of basic Puritan ideas. We have already mentioned Jung's conception of Self, with its implications for a sacred dimension of personal identity. Still more striking is the unexpected revival of the Renaissance ideal of chastity. For Edmund Spenser, an early Puritan poet, chastity was the embodiment of integrity, and he made his strange allegorical poem *The Virgin Queen* a paean to this virtue in Elizabeth I. Half a century later, Milton felt that chastity ought also to be a masculine ideal. The Lady in his allegorical masque *Comus* is an anima figure who welcomes "pure-eyed Faith, white-handed Hope," and the "unblemished form of Chastity" in place of the original Pauline triad of Faith, Hope, and Charity. Replying to a more unbridled Renaissance Spirit, she develops an ethic of austerity:

> . . . do not charge most innocent Nature,
> As if she would her children should be riotous
> With her abundance. She, good cateress,
> Means her provision only to the good,
> That live according to her sober laws
> And hold dictate of spare temperance.
> If every just man that now pines with want
> Had but a moderate and beseeming share
> Of that which lewdly pamper'd luxury
> Now heaps upon some few with vast excess,
> Nature's full blessings would be well dispens'd
> In unsuperfluous even proportion . . .[40]

Milton's Lady later calls this "the sage / And serious doctrine of virginity." This is a vision, beyond social conscience, of integrity itself, a refusal to overemphasize any part for the sake of the sanctity of the whole. A similar austerity is attempted by people in the West today who strive for an ecological consciousness of what and how they consume, but to find a true modern analogue to Milton, we have to look to those who have emerged from the authoritarian regimes of Eastern Europe to speak with conscience for our collective fate. I am thinking of Solzhenitsyn, Sakharov, Milosz, Walesa, and (most recently) Havel. The attitude they display is one which Heinrich Boll has ascribed to Havel: "courtesy towards God." Reviewing the Czech president's prison letters to his wife Olga, Boll writes: "The apparently monastic peace with which he writes from his cell is deceptive. This God seeker who admits his penitence does not complain about his circumstances. He feels bound: the Latin 'religari' means restrained — one of the etymological definitions of religion. . . . Havel's shyness, his courteousness, and his love of order, which has nothing to do with social order policy, all of whose victim he is, together leave no room for demonstrative declarations."[41]

Milton and Havel share in the acceptance of a religious background that binds the moral sense and requires of them an exceptionally pure life. Acknowledging that this austerity is not achieved at the expense of the body or of individuation, but is an authentic expression of masculine wholeness, a Czech colleague of Havel has compared him to a "chaste centaur."[42]

It is an important sign of the Puritan revival in our postmodern time to see the word "chaste" applied to a man. It returns our culture to a central concern with integrity that the Puritans had rescued from an unconscious moral tradition. Prior to the spread of Puritan influence, chastity had been an ideal projected for the most part onto women. Marina Warner describes an allegory of the virtue Chastity, painted on commission by Giovanni Battista Moroni in the mid or later 1550s, which bears the earnest legend: "Castitas infamiae nube obscurat emergit" (Chastity, once obscured by the cloud of slander, comes forth). . . . There is something preposterous, almost appealingly ludicrous about her big, parted marmoreal legs, her naked muscly arms, and the Amazonian undress she wears, her tunic fastened to her neck with a string halter and uncovering her regular, glabrous bosom. She looks trapped by her condition as allegory, forlorn in the unlikelihood of appearance and dress that her emblematic character has necessitated. . . . The improbability of . . . [Moroni's] Chastity distracts the amused viewer from the emblem she tenders on her monumental right knee, which her hands and her proud glance toward us ask us to note: a colander-like sieve, cribbled with regular punctures and yet filled with water.[43]

This sieve "defying all laws of nature" was originally the sign of the Chastity of a Vestal Virgin of Rome, Tuccia. According to Warner, the story is recorded during the first century A.D. both in Pliny's *Natural History* and in Valerius Maximus' *Facta et Dicta Memorabilia* and is later referred to in Augustine's *City of God*.

> Tuccia was accused of breaking her vow of chastity as a priestess of Vesta. To refute the slanderers, and reveal just how chaste she was, she prayed to the goddess and then made her way to the river Tiber. There, panning its waters with a sieve, she filled it to the brim and carried the water back to the temple of Vesta, to offer it to the goddess as the proof of her continence. The very word "continence" reveals the association between the whole unimpaired body of a virtuous person and a virgin, and the sound vessel or container that suffers no puncture or crack; Tuccia's sieve, miraculously made whole by the power of her own wholeness, provides us with a symbol of ideal integrity. . . .[44]

Obviously, even the ancient world was stretching for an archetypal representation of integrity; as Warner points out, this is an impossible image. It becomes a cruel double bind when it is imposed on women as a standard they should somehow embody in their sexual lives. Warner is withering toward the idealizing sexism of the sieve which does not leak.

But Tuccia's sieve is a creative image that conveys the paradoxical essence of integrity as experienced in the subtle body of someone graced to contain a moral process: a miraculous capacity to contain and be open to affect at the same time. Tuccia's sieve has recently taken new life as an image of the analytic container, the ark of the psychotherapy relationship. Since Winnicott, the consulting room has been conceptualized as a transitional space that is chaste but free—a holding environment open to the possibilities of play. Jung's image for this space is the alchemical vessel, both an open retort accepting the flow of archetypal affect from the world and a container "hermetically" sealed by the deity to ensure the containment of the affect undergoing transformation. Analytical psychotherapists have grown used to working within this closed but open space.

Perhaps the problem with the allegory lies less with the paradox of the open container than with the use of water to symbolize what is contained. If the water is, as I think, an attempt to represent unconscious libido or affect, the choice of liquid betrays the primitive assumption that emotion must always overflow into action. It is precisely the contribution of psychotherapy to have discovered that this need not be the case: affect, held with integrity, keeps itself in place. This is why psychotherapists strive for their own version of chastity, through Freud's rule of abstinence, which means at bottom holding the patient's affects with integrity. Psychotherapists disagree violently among themselves about how exactly that is to be done, but on the central point there is a consensus of experience: when psychotherapy is conducted with integrity, the miracle of Tuccia's sieve occurs. The unconscious libido is free to flow, yet stays contained.

This image conceals much of the history of our concept of integrity. In the time of Elizabeth I, who adopted the sieve as her personal emblem, Tuccia's sieve was an allegory of Prudence. Of the classical cardinal virtues, Prudence is the one that comes closest to capturing the elusive essence of integrity. The association of Elizabeth's prudence with her chastity was elaborated by Spenser's *The Faerie Queen*. Though himself a Puritan, Spenser drew upon the medieval Catholic synthesis of classical and Christian virtues that we find in St. Thomas Aquinas. The great Thomistic scholar Josef Pieper has made it clear that for St. Thomas, Prudence was the basis of the other cardinal virtues: justice, fortitude, and temperance.

> Prudence, then, is the mold and mother of all virtues, the circumspect and resolute shaping power of our minds which transforms knowledge of reality into realization of the good. It holds within itself the humility of silent, that is to say, of unbiased perception, the trueness-to-being of memory; the art of receiving counsel; alert, composed readiness for the unexpected. Prudence means the studied seriousness and, as it were, the filter of deliberation, and at the same time the brave boldness to make final decisions. It means purity, straightforwardness, candor, and simplicity of character; it means standing superior to the utilitarian complexities of mere "tactics."[45]

This is a near approach to the idea of integrity, one that tends to exclude the shadow, but is nevertheless suggestive of an attitude by which wholeness might be achieved. It sounds a bit like an ideal description of the analytic attitude, with its stance of evenly suspended, free-floating attention.

As an epigraph to his fine small book on Prudence, Pieper

offers an unexpected line from Matthew (6:22): "If thy eye is single, the whole of thy body will be lit up."[46] Again, this is not only a definition of prudence; it is a demonstration of the power of integrity. In St. Thomas's philosophy, however, *integritas* was not the same thing as prudence. *Integritas* was a condition, not a moral attitude; it referred to the wholeness of the image of God, and to what was made in God's image, like the body that would be resurrected entire after death and like ideal works of art. Applied to the beauty of art, *integritas* signified things made in such a way that the relation of their parts to each other imitated the proportions of nature and participated in the wholeness of God.[47] *Integritas* was also, as we have seen, the human condition before the Fall, a condition of being without inclination to sin; works made with *integritas* helped to return human beings to an original state of likeness to God. But Aquinas stopped well short of suggesting that *integritas* could be an aim in what a person did in day-to-day life. It was not until the time of the Puritans, when Milton said that someone who wanted to write good poetry "ought himself to be a true poem" that the idea of a life having the integrity of a work of art took hold.[48]

The word "integrity" is not to be found in Chaucer and only sparingly in Shakespeare, where it does not stand out.[49] It appears in a few highly significant places in the 1611 King James Bible, the translation that culminated a half-century of Puritan pressure upon the crown for a high-quality English version of the scriptures that could be read, preached from, and studied by individuals and which became the most widely read book of all time. In Genesis, the book of Job, the Proverbs, and the Psalms, "integrity" is used to translate Hebrew words that convey the Judaic notion of living in accord with God's law by sticking to a virtuous way of life. Integrity is associated in these contexts with purity, holiness, and uprightness, and the image evoked is of a human being struggling to live by the divine will. Like uprightness, a concept we can trace to the Egyptians and the Sumerians,[50] integrity implied a human standpoint, the ethical attempt to live in accord with a God-granted nature. In Milton's time, there was a return to this Old Testament notion of an ethical stance, one that accepted God as the living, limiting ground of moral choice. The prudent sieve of Christian faith now became integrity, an attitude of free choice that managed nonetheless to contain, and miraculously obey, the will of God. The Puritans had succeeded in transforming a Catholic doctrine of salvation into a Protestant ethic of conscience.

DIALOGUE WITH SHAME

In our time, psychotherapeutic dialogue has become a new cultural image of integrity. Perhaps that explains the vigor with which we are presently defending its sanctity, its privacy, its chastity, and its sheltering frame. Such conscientiousness is a form of Puritanism, as Guggenbühl-Craig has said, but rather than condemn it as a perversion of the archetype of purity, we might welcome it as a revival of an image of integrity that dropped away after the Puritans, one that we need to heal our moral process. We can perhaps find in the Puritanical attempts to regulate our field an effort to reassert a prudent single-mindedness in the way we go about caring for our patients.

What psychotherapy has been struggling to recover, I think, is the understanding of a moral process that is free, yet binding in its acceptance of a higher authority. This paradox is expressed in the language of analytical psychology as the relation of ego to Self and is conveyed in such slogans of the Twelve Step programs as "Let go and let God."

Recently, my colleague Andrew Samuels has made a helpful theoretical contribution to this essential dynamic of integrity. Samuels explains that conscience is an interplay between two psychological faculties, one that he calls original morality and another which he terms the moral imagination. Havel's "quiet restlessness" impressed Heinrich Boll; the original morality is the "quiet" and the moral imagination the "restlessness."[51] In *Paradise Lost,* this pair is God and Satan. Original morality is "some kind of innate moral sense," but, as Samuels points out: "insufficient for the leading of a moral life; it can be experienced as harsh, vengeful, primitive and cold. In an adult, original morality can take the form of a profound suspiciousness of others, a tendency to jump to the worst possible conclusions, to rejoice in the other's misery when it seems deserved, and, ultimately, to retreat into the wilderness to feed on locusts and honey."[52]

This is surely a good description of Puritanism at its worst, belief in God as an endless occasion for guilt. Moral imagination, by contrast is the "means by which we consider complex social and political issues." Milton's unforgettable image of Satan summoning all the gods of antiquity like so many fallen angels to decide how to interfere in God's newest creation, man, emphasizes how central a role the shadow plays in such deliberations. Samuels's own example of the nihilism implicit in the moral imagination is the prayer read at the start of the Jewish Day of Atonement service:

> All vows, bonds, devotions, promises, obligations, penalties and oaths: wherewith we have vowed, sworn, devoted and bound ourselves: from this Day of Atonement unto the next Day of Atonement; lo, all these, we repent us in them. They shall be absolved, released, annulled, made void, and of none effect: they shall not be binding nor shall they have any power. Our vows shall not be vows: our bonds shall not be bonds: and our oaths shall not be oaths.[53]

The Yom Kippur prayer, as Samuels points out, cancels resolutions "at the very moment of making them" indicating that "a recognition of the unlivable nature of original morality on its own lies at the heart even of Judaism," the religion which is "so often unfairly castigated . . . as the source of repressive and legalistic moralism." The paradoxical prayer epitomizes moral imagination because it "contains an intuitive and psychological understanding of what a moral principle really is," for example, that it is sometimes "morally permissible to tell lies," "to break promises," and to refuse to give help. Moral imagination is characterized by "forgiveness, and not blame." And moral imagination "typically requires a weighing of conflicting claims."[54] (One thinks of the long discussion of conflicting obligations in Cicero's *De Officiis*.)

It is the capacity to articulate the relation between original morality and moral imagination that concerns us, a capacity that rare figures like Havel and Milton model for us. As Samuels puts it, "moral imagination enables us effectively to use original morality; original morality guarantees the depth and authenticity of moral imagination." Both "are equally archetypal; both have to become personal and express themselves in human relationships at all stages of life. . . . Neither is divine; if it lies anywhere, divinity lies in their conclave."[55] Their conclave is what a developed Puritan sensibility would have meant by integrity, and we recover the archetype of purity when we engage in an authentic moral process. Experiencing, if only for a brief time, the radical chastity of a Milton or a Havel, we feel pure: our shadow is fully disclosed to us against a background of strict accountability, and everything in our nature is introduced, with courtesy, to God.

Without a conception of God, it is quite hard for us today to experience our original morality without anxiety, and harder still to bring it into relation to the moral imagination. Many people today are content to use the two moralities as separate systems of their moral vehicle, the moral imagination as an accelerator and the original morality as the brake. Freud even reified this dualism of the Liberal psyche with his depiction of id and superego, and we can see the extreme of this splitting in the parallel Machiavellianism and stern morality of a cautionary figure like Richard Nixon. Nixon's failure lies not on either pole of moral process (on both he is spectacular) but in their integration, and rightly do we miss in him the integrity that could have been occasioned by their conclave. He is an extreme victim of our culture's fear of the Puritan attempt to bring these systems into relation, but he is a mythic figure for us because he shows us how by separating them we can cast integrity itself into shadow. As it stands, those in our culture most likely to find the full measure of their integrity are those who are less defended against accepting the shadow in which integrity nowadays is likely to reside. These are particularly people in psychotherapy and in the Twelve Step programs. It was not always so, and our anxiety in the face of our integrity's vulnerability has all the overtones of a depression over a lost object.

If we could find our way back to the Puritan calm of Milton, one of our discoveries might be a far greater capacity than we have at present to accept shame. Learning to accept shame was the psychological point of the Puritan emphasis on original sin, and it is the moral achievement of Milton's Adam in *Paradise Lost*. There Adam tells Eve:

> What better can we do, than to the place
> Repairing where he judg'd us, prostrate fall
> Before him reverent, and there confess
> Humbly our faults, and pardon beg, with tears
> Watering the ground, and with our sighs the Air

> Frequenting, sent from hearts contrite, in sign
> Of sorrow unfeigned, and humiliation meek.[56]

Contrition is an image that our culture has lost with the decline of Christianity. One of our best moral artists, Woody Allen, has made more than one black comedy out of the idea that contrition can do little for a non-Christian, and of the fact that for many today the choice is between acceptance of guilt and acceptance of sociopathy. Yet if we try to rediscover the healthy Puritan attitude toward shame, we quickly get bogged down in the New England Puritans' much greater emphasis on guilt, which produced a complete distrust of individual initiative and the anima. Jungian psychology recognizes this excessive distrust of people doing what they like as an attitude of the *senex,* the restrictive negative father. In American culture, our failure to find a healthy father has been a major national wound, and our sense that the Puritans stand in our way is one reason we can't trust them as a guide to our psychological development.

To get to the right attitude toward shame, we might follow the suggestion of Robert Neville and inform the Puritan understanding of responsibility with the Confucian, turning to the Chinese culture because it has not confounded shame with guilt. That this is a good way to understand Milton's sincerity is perhaps the suggestion of Marx's comparing him to a "silkworm" and Eliot's disparaging of his poetry as a "Chinese wall." It may be that what is most characteristic in Milton's point of view, and what we need still to learn from, is more compatible with Chinese culture than our own.

In the hexagram of the *I Ching* that we have already quoted—Hexagram 12, "Standstill"—there is a line translated by Richard Wilhelm and Cary Baynes as "They bear shame." I am told by a student of Chinese philosophy that his teacher translates this line "They embrace shame." How far we are in American culture today from this attitude! The Wilhelm-Baynes commentary on this line reads: "Inferior people who have risen to power illegitimately do not feel equal to the responsibility they have taken upon themselves. In their hearts they begin to be ashamed, although at first they do not show it outwardly. This marks a turn for the better."[57]

Early in my life, I shared with many other Americans the power of such a turning point. It came when I was nearly fifteen, during the Army-McCarthy hearings, after four long years in which (to quote Doris Lessing): "In America the hysteria had grown till that great nation looked from outside like a dog driven mad by an infestation of fleas, snapping and biting at its own flesh; and a man called Joe McCarthy, who had no qualities at all, save one, the capacity to terrorise other people, was able to do as he liked."[58]

During this "sensational, nationally televised, 36-day hearing on his charges of subversion against army officers and civilian officials,"[59] Joseph Welch asked the senator from Wisconsin a famous question: "Senator, have you no shame?" I doubt very much that at that moment Senator McCarthy "began to be ashamed," but I do know that at that moment the American people began to be ashamed for him, and ashamed of themselves for letting him get so far. In the unconscious, the McCarthy era was over—as it was in fact within nine months, when he was not only retired as chairman of the investigating committee but "condemned" by the Senate for conduct "contrary to Senate traditions."[60] For myself, America became, for the first time since my childhood, a place where one could breathe again. I felt a similar lift nineteen years later, in May, 1973, when the Select Committee on Presidential Campaign Activities under Sen. Samuel J. Ervin, Jr., began televised public hearings on the planning of the Watergate break-in.

I think psychology would do well to become more interested in the attitude that enables us to "embrace shame"—and in the relief we experience emotionally when we do. For in these emotions we discover the peculiar relationship of integrity to the shadow. One could almost speak of stages of integrity, advancing the relation to the shadow. An initial stage is denial that there is shadow (the McCarthy era, Nixon's overwhelming landslide victory in 1972 a few months after the actual Watergate break-in); a turning-point stage is the acceptance of shadow (the recognition of abuse of authority by McCarthy, by Nixon); a final stage is a sense of restored wholeness once the "full disclosure" of the shadow has been integrated. I believe this to be a dialectic of integrity, proceeding through the shadow.

This dialectic is not an easy path for collectives. Neither has our collective psychology made it easy for individuals to take the path of embracing shame. Only recently, in fact, has psychology itself "embraced shame" as a topic for sustained inquiry. The first book of essays devoted to a range of psychological views on shame was not published until 1987.[61]

When I was in medical school I was taught a Freudian view of shame by my psychiatry professors. They explained that the superego, the part of our "mental apparatus" formed as a consequence of our early socialization at the hands of parents, has two sectors: the conscience and the ego-ideal. Guilt was said to be the emotional consequence of any failure to live up to the dictates of conscience; shame, the result of failures to live up to the ego-ideal.[62] In its development, shame was thought to be earlier than guilt, taking origin in the period of toilet training, Freud's famous "anal phase." Recognizing this time as belonging to the stage of increased toddler activity, Erik Erikson had expanded this developmental period as a time characterized by conflict of "autonomy versus shame and doubt." Erikson's description of this developmental stage is classic and should be read in its entirety. I will quote only one brief passage here to convey the flavor of what influenced me, clinically, at the time:

> Outer control at this stage, therefore, must be firmly reassuring. The infant must come to feel that the basic faith in existence, which is the lasting treasure saved from the rages of the oral stage, will not be jeopardized by this about-face of his, this sudden violent wish to have a choice, to appropriate demandingly, and to eliminate stubbornly. Firmness must protect him against the potential anarchy of his as yet untrained sense of discrimination, his inability to hold on and to let go with discretion. As his environment encourages him to "stand on his own feet," it must protect him against meaningless and arbitrary experiences of shame and of early doubt.
>
> The latter danger is the one best known to us. For if denied the gradual and well-guided experience of the autonomy of free choice (or if, indeed, weakened by an initial loss of trust) the child will turn against himself all his urge to discriminate and to manipulate. He will overmanipulate himself, he will develop a precocious conscience.[63]

Like many other budding psychiatrists of my generation, I vowed never to let this happen when the child in my patients resurfaced as part of treatment and I had my chance to re-parent the toddler who had been so mishandled the first time around. As a consequence, I spent almost the first twenty years of my clinical work helping my patients overcome their shame. I developed a well-deserved reputation for making my patients feel better. Less than ten years ago, I began to realize that all along I had been unconsciously colluding with an attitude in them that shame is something to be ashamed of. It occurred to me that by doing so, I was interfering with part of my patients' opportunity to exercise their integrity. I realize now that I had misread Erikson's meaning when he said, "Too much shaming does not lead to genuine propriety but to a secret determination to try to get away with things, unseen — if, indeed, it does not result in defiant shamelessness."[64]

I had taken Erikson's warning naively as an indictment of the undermining negative mother. My later reading, in Jungian training, of Neumann and Henderson and von Franz convinced me that the negative mother ruled over the late pre-Oedipal period, and that my duty was to get everyone past the negative mother and onto the subsequent father stage, where they could reach the benefits of an Oedipal-level identity.[65] You will see that this is a Jungianized version of a stereotyped Freudian idea, helping the patients get over their fear of the father. Although it was clear that these same patients had shadow problems that I also hoped they would face, I thought first I had to free them of shame so that they would be able to handle the necessary guilt. To do this, I had to be careful to lower the inhumanly high standard, which the negative mother's animus had set up, like a bar too high for her child to jump over. All this demanding ego-ideal had done, I thought, was to inhibit autonomy and lower self-esteem.

After my Jungian training, however, I began to be exposed to the revisionist psychoanalytic thinking of Heinz Kohut, who reformulated much of the territory that had been secured under the rubric of "ego ideal."[66] Kohut spoke of a basic unconscious structure, which he called the self, with two poles — the grandiose exhibitionistic self and the idealized parental imago. We can see these sides of the self as carrying the conflict, between the child's autonomy, on the one hand, and shame and doubt, on the other, which Erikson had postulated for the second pre-Oedipal stage. But by reformulating the ego-ideal as the idealized parental imago and making it part of the self, Kohut invited us to reconsider the need to set up ideals and find ways of living with them. Kohut's idea was that the child would merge the ideal part of its selfhood with a parent who stood for something. Although Kohut himself did not say so, the clear implication is that shame is the letdown that comes when the ideal is unable to find an anchor in the parent, either because the parent fails to incarnate ideal ways, or because the child is made to feel unworthy of participation in the parent's ideal qualities.[67] In the view of self-psychology, then, shame is the crisis that emerges when the ideal aspirations of the self founder.[68]

In a careful analysis of shame as one of the "emotions of self-assessment" alongside pride and guilt, Gabriele Taylor has explained that "it is its relation to integrity which makes shame such a potentially devastating emotion. . . . In shame the self is seen as less worthy than the agent thought, assumed, or hoped he was or might become; such thoughts, hopes or assumptions have now turned out to be unfounded."[69]

Yet surviving such experiences is part of our growth. Jungian analysts have conceived Freud's oral stage of development as encircled by the image of the nursing pair, the archetypal Great Mother with her Divine Child, while the anal stage is disrupted by the pitched battle between the negative mother and her enfant terrible. This latter strife proceeds, Halloween-style, between a mythological witch and trickster, in a drama of manipulation and countermanipulation which uses shame as an emotional currency. If the witch mother makes the price she exacts in shame a condition of the child's continued freedom, the trickster infant counters by devaluing the currency itself. Erikson understood that "there is a limit to a child's and an adult's endurance in the face of demands to consider himself, his body, and his wishes as evil and dirty, and to his belief in the infallibility of those who pass such judgment. He may be apt to turn things around, and to consider as evil only the fact that they exist: his chance will come when they are gone, or when he will go from them."[70]

The problem for the therapist in trying to help patients caught in this revenge-seeking, sociopathic style is not to collude with the patients in denying validity to the currency of shame through which they must purchase their self-esteem, but to help with the acceptance of sorrow that things have come to this pass, showing the patients that this very ruefulness is their ticket of return to a more human way of relating. Such experiences prepare for a genuine remorse over the destructiveness of shadow, and the possibility of atonement by change in behavior.

Enduring both our humiliation at being less than we thought and our sense of floundering in the absence of an ideal orientation forces upon us a rudimentary feeling for the integrity of what remains. It is this integrity which supplies a core of self-esteem that gives us courage for a new attempt to merge with the ideal and restore self-respect.

The acceptance by the self of its own failures to achieve its ideals is the only way that it can earn the empathy required for a human attitude toward the shadow. When the shadow appears to act out what has been morally repressed, it is as if another self emerges, out of relation to the ideals in which we normally center our identity. That self does things we know are wrong and yet for which we must assume responsibility, creating the anxiety we know as guilt. Taylor explains that guilt, like shame, has consequences for the self: "Guilt . . . too is related to integrity, though the perceived threat to integrity takes here a different form. When feeling guilt, . . . the agent sees himself as the doer of a wicked deed and so as alien to himself. He sees another self emerging. The 'wicked deed' refers to his action (or omission) seen as violating some taboo, and the emerging self is the self capable of violating the taboo."[71]

But simply taking responsibility for the shadow, like Dr. Jekyll paying for the damages of Mr. Hyde, does nothing to heal the split between the two selves. To see the shadow as something more than a moral alien over which we must stand guard, and to realize that we are dealing with an inner companion whose feelings and values might be approached psychologically, tests our capacity to empathize with a self that falls short. This capacity is developed through our own experiences of shame.

These considerations have reoriented my clinical stance toward shame. I agree with Andrew Morrison that for any individual with major deficits of the self, shame, not rage, is the principal affect.[72] Rage in all its forms from resentment to revenge is often a shadow reaction to the frustration of not knowing what to do with shame, and there will be little integration of the shadow if shame is not first addressed. I have learned to take seriously times in the therapy when the patient and I share, usually nonverbally, a feeling of humiliation. Perhaps I am regretting a failure of empathy, containment, or imagination in relation to what has been presented to me. My patient may be feeling discouragement in the ability to communicate honestly or a lack of real commitment to the work. In the shame of such moments, I work hard to hold the feeling of failure until we both have acknowledged and mourned our mutual betrayal of the ideal. The paradox has been that sharing the shame of the lost opportunity has been at least as healing as the happier moments when we have been able to be together as ideal analyst and ideal analysand.

All of this I think John Milton understood perfectly as his relation to God. The Puritan doctrine of sin, contrition, and penitence was a psychology of healing through shame. What we have today is a memory of guilt without a sense of shame to enable us to process it.[73]

We must let shame have its place in the ecology of integrity. Its soil does not dishonor the consulting room any more than sin desecrates a religion of redemption. We are dealing here with a basic pair of opposites belonging to integrity, which Mary Douglas has called Purity and Danger. In her book by that title, "an analysis of the concepts of pollution and taboo," she points out that "religions often sacralise the very unclean things which have been rejected with abhorrence."[74] Jung has demonstrated with his "Transformation Symbolism in the Mass" how packed religious rituals are with the symbolism of individuation.[75] We should follow Douglas's lead in recognizing the role that shameful things play in our notions of sacred purity. The great Christian ritual of communion involves accepting into our bodies a mortifying piece of evidence—the flesh and blood of the savior defiled and stripped of life by human cruelty.

Shame also figures in the cementing of intimacy in marriage. Possibly the most moving scene I have ever witnessed in a motion picture occurs in F. W. Murnau's silent film *Sunrise*, where a simple farmer, crazed by his love for a city woman, is driven to try to kill his wife. He lifts his oar to strike her as he is rowing their wooden boat toward the shore of the city. She sees what he intends, and he stops himself. His remorse is so great that she is moved to forgive him; touched by her forgiveness he falls in love with her again. When they arrive in the city, it is as partners in a conscious marriage.

The paradox depicted here also touches the inner marriage of individuals trying to get along with themselves: the shadow that threatens to disintegrate the personality is the occasion for the shame that allows it to consolidate at a higher level of moral development. Such shame is healing only if it is held with integrity. The alchemical name for holding shame with integrity is *mortificatio,* the rot of human chemicals in a closed container — truly a mortifying experience. T. S. Eliot's *The Waste Land,* written in the disillusioned wake of World War I, is a classic presentation of a cultural *mortificatio.* In an analysis of that poem, Patricia Berry points to the healing effect of Eliot's ability to sustain a concentrated focus on his culture's impurity: "Eliot's *Waste Land* ends with *Shantih, shantih, shantih* — a feeling of pure but hard-earned peace. These final lines of *Shantih* ring with such beauty, integrity — and virginity — because of the extraordinary impurity of the poem that has preceded; the 'heap of broken images,' the 'wrinkled dugs,' the rat 'dragging its slimy belly on the bank' — a teeming richness of complex, sophisticated impurity that readies us for a piece of integrity."[76]

Significantly, this comes at the end of the poem. Erikson has postulated that integrity of this kind — what Christian culture would have thought of as the integrity of God in response to the effort at integrity by a man or woman — is generally reserved for the end of life. In the late works of great artists, we can find abundant evidence for this entry into the grace of *integritas.* W. B. Yeats's *The Circus Animals' Desertion* was written in the last year of his life, and as Berry once again points out, it reveals another final evidence of a poet's purification, the capacity for pure image itself. This poem's last stanza reads:

> Those masterful images because complete
> Grew in pure mind but out of what began?
> A mound of refuse or the sweepings of a street,
> Old kettles, old bottles, and a broken can,
> Old iron, old bones, old rags, that raving slut
> Who keeps the till. Now that my ladder's gone
> I must lie down here where all the ladders start
> In the foul rag and bone shop of the heart.[77]

As Berry puts it: "The pure of which Yeats speaks would seem the virginal achievement of image. The mound of refuse, the raving slut, the foul rag-and-bone shop of the heart are the impurities that give integrity to the virginity of the image."[78]

Our psychological age is just beginning to create an image of moral process that has a similar wholeness. We are still in the process of learning that integrity is achieved by an openness to the impure on the one hand and a participation in the pure on the other and that we cannot afford to leave out either pole. We have told ourselves that earlier periods had far less tolerance for shadow than we do and that we are therefore morally more mature. It may be nearer the mark to say that our forebears had less anxiety than we do in accepting a standard by which what is pure and what is impure might be judged. If anything, our moral process is not as close to consciousness as theirs. Our moral sense seems best to express itself nowadays in symptoms like shame and anxiety, and psychotherapy has been right to realize that we need to befriend these symptoms of integrity with the attention and respect that is their due.

3

Integrity and Gender

IN HIS DISCUSSION of basic notions of good, Alasdair MacIntyre suggests that we compare "the very different lists of items which different authors in different times and places have included in their catalogues of virtues."[1] Applying this method to Western literature, he argues, we might contrast the qualities espoused as worthy of emulation by Homer, Aristotle, the New Testament, Benjamin Franklin, and Jane Austen. In context, this last name is surprising. Homer, MacIntyre reminds us, emphasized the excellences of the warrior: courage, cunning, and physical strength. Aristotle demanded the civic attributes of magnanimity, munificence, good judgment, and the capacity for friendship. The New Testament created an ideal of service to God through the virtues of faith, hope, charity, and humility. Puritan cleanliness, silence, and industry were added by Benjamin Franklin as part of an ethic of mercantile success. Jane Austen, however, seemed to seize on integrity and to shift its meaning by suggesting to a propertied class that it ought to gentrify itself into persons of amiability, constancy, and self-knowledge.[2]

In the nineteenth century, the evolution implied might have sounded simply like a history of social progress, but today we are likely to regard Austen's accomplishment as a move from masculine to feminine notions of virtue. We appreciate the dry groundedness with which she promotes her ideals through the "sense and sensibility" of her novels, which seem to take the problem of integrity not only into daily life, but to how people actually relate to how they live.

The fiction Austen pioneered tests the consistency of a point of view against the realities of society, and we still read the kind of novel she introduced. The reading of novels and its closely derived activity, the watching of movies, have changed irrevocably our notions of what integrity is, getting us to regard integrity as an aspect of personal being. For us, integrity is part of the genuine interest in others that Austen called "amiability" and of the continuity of identity in caring that she called "constancy."

We still judge the people we meet in literature and films by how well they meet these standards. The film *Driving Miss Daisy* turns on the degree to which Miss Daisy's discovery of amiability endangers the perverse constancy of the acerbic character by which we recognize her. But the notion of integrity we get from fiction depends less on precepts applied to experience than on allegiance to experience itself; it appeals to a part of ourselves that likes to be shown rather than told what the story of a life means. This part of us has an endless appetite for the recitation of everyday mysteries and a deep appreciation of the comedy and pathos of life's refusal to follow principle. And this part is fascinated with relationships, the relation of individuals to themselves, to each other, and to society. As Nancy Hale asserts in her book *The Realities of Fiction,* "Relationship is . . . the proper concern of the novel," and it has become as well the satisfaction accorded by enduring films.[3]

Following a modern habit of giving what we like in ourselves a gender linkage, we have assigned this way of receiving and considering experience to the feminine. Jane Austen's concern for people who are going about the business of forming relationships seems to us a feminine consciousness, and not just because she is a woman. A similar consciousness turns up in Henry James and E. M. Forster and seems feminine in them. We delight in the patterns that it is able to disclose to us. Where speaking and doing might be masculine, we feel such listening and watching to be feminine, and to support an integrity all its own.

We also believe that the practice of psychotherapy requires this receptive style. Since Winnicott, analysts have favored a style of working that depends upon receptive holding of the patient's material. An actively engaged interest that does not seek to interfere with the patient's own affective track is now seen as preferable even to interpretation. Barbara Stevens Sullivan has called this attitude "psychotherapy grounded in the feminine principle."[4]

Much psychotherapy time is spent restoring, and enjoying, the capacity to move with the flow of experience, and psychotherapy can become a narrative without more point than the restoration of the person's capacity to live it through. This way of bearing with experience with integrity, rather than finding a way to act upon it with integrity, amounts to a new heroic ideal, and it is one that many today associate with the feminine.

Those who make this gender assumption are not necessarily followers of Jung; the idea that being with, rather than doing to, is the feminine way of integrity has a venerable history, one that enters the modern era through the novels of Jane Austen. It is presented most persuasively in Austen's final novel, which we know by the appropriate name Austen's brother gave it after her death: *Persuasion*. The heroine of this book, Anne Elliot, is persuaded by a friend of the family to break off an engagement with the man she loves because he is only a navy lieutenant, with slight apparent financial prospects, and Anne's father, a widowed baronet, is exceedingly vain about family expectations.

The lieutenant withdraws in wounded pride, and though he rather quickly becomes a captain, building up his fortunes to the point that he would be an entirely suitable husband to Anne, he cannot bring himself to approach her again for eight and a half years, in which time her youthful bloom fades. Eventually, however, he is drawn into the periphery of her family circle again by becoming involved in the courtship of one of her cousins. Anne, who misses nothing, holds in consciousness the feelings of all the people around her, as well as her own and his, until he can bring himself to confess that he is still, after all, in love with her. Their eventual marriage is achieved in a way that is entirely satisfactory to the social circle that at first would vehemently have opposed it.

The point of the novel is the integrity of Anne's ability to sense and lovingly contain the feelings of the members of her kinship group while continuing to honor her own emotional position; she is a model for a self-fulfillment which is ecologically sound. Her ability to maintain amiability alongside constancy is extraordinary especially because her moral level — above all, her self-knowledge — is so much higher than that of the people around her. Her triumph of love over vanity is more than the transcendence of a genuine feeling for people over the narcissistic style of an insecure gentry; it is the individuation of a sensibility guided by constancy in relationship. To let relationship slip from consciousness, for Austen's heroine, "would not be in the nature of any woman who truly loved."[5]

A gendered conception of integrity is assailable on both political and empirical grounds, but it can be helpful, offering a way to discriminate aspects of integrity that a neutral conception might leave out. That there is a discrete "feminine" style of integrity is an important idea in Jungian psychology, where something very like Austen's feminine notion of constancy in relationship has a role in the discovery of the Self, the objective constancy of the personality. We cannot appreciate Jung's fundamental contribution to the study of integrity without recognizing that, like Jane Austen, he organizes his conception through his understanding of the feminine. In other words, like Austen, he gets to the idea of integrity itself in a gender-assigning mode.

A way to find the common thread uniting the female novelist of conscious sensibility and the male psychologist of unconscious wisdom is the emphasis both of them place on *wholeness* as the organizing principle of a human life. This holistic sense becomes the basis of the ethical stance for both Austen and Jung. Like our modern idea of ecology, which has the Gaia hypothesis behind it,[6] it is a notion grounded in the mythology of the feminine, and with strongly matriarchal overtones implying the point of view of a consciously good mother. Wholeness is what Alasdair MacIntyre calls "the good of a human life conceived as a unity."[7]

In *Persuasion,* Anne Elliot seems to be compensating for the early loss of her mother and the subsequent damage to her family and friends at the hands of a supercilious father, by finding her way to a conscious femininity that can take care of the people around her. Jane Austen, by contrast, seems to have had a family that was constantly supportive to her. Creating characters in the round, with a sense of their social circle, and emphasizing the continuity of their individual narratives as lived, morally, in the world were her chief concerns as an artist. The resulting image of a closed circle, so often applied to her fiction, is not without resonance to the earliest idea of the breast. In Jung's thought, too, the image of the Self, with its round mandala symbolism and its conception of a preexisting wholeness that embraces personal identity, has strong overtones of the sensibility of a healthy mother.

Psychologically, the mother is first preserver of the unity

of life, and it is just this sense of unity that Jane Austen emphasizes with her stress on "constancy," which is for her (according to MacIntyre) "a virtue the possession of which is a prerequisite for the possession of other virtues."[8] MacIntyre believes that Austen is "the last great effective imaginative voice in the tradition of thought about, and practice of, the virtues"; she "turns away from the competing catalogues of the virtues of the eighteenth century and restores a teleological perspective."[9] In terms that remind us of Jung, MacIntyre insists on the importance of an overriding purpose, for

> unless there is a *telos* which transcends the limited goods of [moral] practices by constituting the good of a whole human life, the good of a human life conceived as a unity, it will *both* be the case that a certain subversive arbitrariness will invade the moral life *and* that we shall be unable to specify the context of certain virtues adequately. These two considerations are reinforced by a third: that there is at least one virtue recognized by the tradition which cannot be specified at all except with reference to the wholeness of a human life — the virtue of integrity or constancy. "Purity of heart," said Kierkegaard, "is to will one thing." This notion of singleness of purpose in a whole life can have no application unless that of a whole life does.[10]

Jane Austen had been exposed, through her reading, to philosophical ideas of the good life (Gilbert Ryle claims that her reading of Shaftesbury made her an Aristotelian),[11] but from her perspective as a novelist, the idea of constancy conveyed the narrative unity of a life. It was a virtue closely allied with self-knowledge in her most developed characters. The moral attitude transformed her relationship to storytelling as surely as the religious attitude transformed Milton's vocation as a poet. In Austen's case, it made her fiction the quintessential expression of a feminine view of integrity. That view is summed up in her word constancy, which MacIntyre places in historical context:

> When Kierkegaard contrasted the ethical and aesthetic ways of life in *Enten-Eller,* he argued that the aesthetic life is one in which a human life is dissolved into a series of separate present moments, in which the unity of a human life disappears from view. By contrast in the ethical life the commitments and responsibilities to the future springing from past episodes in which obligations were conceived and debts assumed unite the present to past and to future in such a way as to make of a human life a unity. . . . By the time Jane Austen writes [in the early nineteenth century] that unity can no longer be treated as a mere presupposition or context for a virtuous life. It has itself to be constantly reaffirmed and its reaffirmation in deed rather than in word is the virtue which Jane Austen calls constancy.[12]

Austen does manage, through the persuasive voice and example of her Anne Elliot, to convince us, as MacIntyre puts it, that constancy "is a virtue which women are more apt to practise than are men."[13] The point carries despite vigorous protest from some of Austen's male characters.

This idea of wholeness or unbroken continuity as a centrally feminine virtue—one that is, like a good mother, both the a priori and the sine qua non of all other virtues—has a long tradition in Western thought. Indeed, it is one of the roots of patriarchal sexism, as Marina Warner has shown in her trilogy of books on the history of gender stereotypes, *Alone of All Her Sex, Joan of Arc,* and *Monuments and Maidens.* In a less conscious period for the feminine, when women had not yet found their voice and men were projecting their own need for anima integrity[14] onto them as a wholesale demand for literal virginity and chastity, women were forced into embodying wholeness and continuity in their concrete physical lives, living out the anima ideal in ways that were stultifying for their individuation. Just as Milton, in claiming chastity as a virtue for men, was taking a step in reclaiming the anima projection, Austen, in claiming constancy for women was rescuing a conscious feminine value from this obscuring tradition of idealization, one that had treacherously resulted in the frequent charge of fickleness being leveled at women whose behavior might seem to disappoint the ideal.

But the virgin archetype, for all its dangers when used as a projective identification, had also been a way of formulating personal and moral integrity. In the Christian allegorical tradition of personification, *Virginitas* became, according to Marina Warner, the sine qua non of a virtue's being a virtue in the first place. Like *Integritas,* which seems to have no tradition of allegorical personification, she tells us that

> virginity itself is rarely represented as a virtue on its own, though obsessively lauded in Christian writing of the early and medieval church. . . . Virginity signified the specific and physical state of bodily integrity resulting from sexual innocence. . . . It could be argued that Mary, the pattern of virginity in her miraculous body (*virgo in partu* as well as at Jesus' conception), and the exemplar of elected chastity, represented the associated virtues sufficiently to impress their importance on believers; but this does not really provide an answer to the startling omission of Virginitas from the canonical lists and tables.

> A reason could be that sexual abstinence and the conquest of carnal passions, symbolized by virginity, are so fundamental to Christian ethics that they are understood to be intrinsic to each virtue; certainly, in the handbooks, like Cesare Ripa's famous *Iconologia,* which . . . systematized the representation of abstract ideas in the seventeenth and eighteenth centuries, the female figures who body forth Faith, and Hope, Prudence, Justice, Fortitude and Temperance and so on, are

understood to be virginal, issuing from the godhead, espoused to him, as chaste and dedicated brides, without issue, monads of primal integrity like Athena. Virginitas herself does appear in Ripa's *Iconologia,* as a typical maiden, garlanded, pale and slender, with a lamb beside her. She is as it were the dressmaker's dummy, on which the patterns of other Virtues are all cut differently.[15]

The weight of these traditions is that it is only with a developed feminine viewpoint that integrity can take on a life and identity of its own. Jung concurs: he never ceased to pay homage to the feminine figures, both inner and outer, who helped him toward his conception of the unity of personality. From his own deeply split mother, who introduced him to the problem of warring opposites, to the inner realization of the gnostic Sophia, who presided as *anima mundi* over his final, alchemical conception of the unity of psyche and world in the *unus mundus,* female figures were the monitors and guides of Jung's attempts at integrity. Helly Preiswerk, Sabina Spielrein, Antonia (Toni) Wolff, and Christiana Morgan played an incalculable role in his formulation of complexes, shadow, anima, and Self, and the ambiguous moral atmosphere surrounding his relationships with each of these women sharpened Jung's interest in an integrity that could comprehend and contain a man's experience of the feminine. Jung's inner explorations led him to confront an anima figure even more difficult than the Dalila that Milton presents in his late verse drama, *Samson Agonistes.*

Jung's first active imaginations—those descents into his own unconscious depths while consciously daydreaming—led him to meet none other than a blind Salome, who seemed to symbolize the intense moods and blind passions Jung was so often subject to, in a life punctuated by rages and crushes. Jung may be the first serious ethical thinker to have found integrity through honoring this kind of anima figure and making an effort to see what she had to tell him. He learned that beside Salome stood Elijah, the figure of the moral prophet who angrily insisted on the idea of God to a forgetful people. In other words, Jung's anima problem (which was enormous — at the time of these imaginations, he had broken with Freud in a rage and was plunged into a marital crisis as well, having decided to accept his former patient Toni Wolff as a lover) led him to a recognition of the psychological need for constancy, which Jung only gradually was to discover in his centering conception of the Self, the eventual God of his own system. This was a discovery of what abides through all inner journeying, and he saw individuation as a progressive capacity to feel and touch its essence. Integrity became for Jung a matter of letting this innermost core of personality have its way.

Describing "the course of development in patients who quietly, and as if unconsciously, outgrew themselves," Jung noted:

> I saw that their fates had something in common. The new thing came to them from obscure possibilities either outside or inside themselves; they accepted it and grew with its help. It seemed to me typical that some took the new thing from outside themselves, others from inside; or rather, that it grew into some persons from without, and into others from within. But the new thing never came exclusively either from within or from without. If it came from outside, it became a profound inner experience; if it came from inside, it became an outer happening. In no case was it conjured into existence intentionally or by conscious willing, but rather seemed to be borne along on the stream of time. . . .
>
> What did these people do in order to bring about the development that set them free? As far as I could see they did nothing . . . [here he quotes the Taoist notion of *wu wei*, doing by not doing] but let things happen. . . . The art of letting things happen, action through non-action, letting go of oneself as taught by Meister Eckhart, became for me the

key that opens the door to the way. We must be able to let things happen in the psyche. For us, this is an art of which most people know nothing. Consciousness is forever interfering, helping, correcting, and negating, never leaving the psychic process to grow in peace.[16]

I believe that like constancy, this conception of integrity is feminine, although it can be grasped by men as well as women. It depends upon an acceptance of a preexisting wholeness and continuity that reflects basic trust of the mother archetype. Those with a conscious connection to the mother principle will take naturally to this conception of integrity. In our patriarchal culture, however, integrity is more usually regarded as an effort expended to find a just accord with nature.

During the past ten years, Carol Gilligan and her group at the Center for the Study of Gender, Education and Human Development at the Harvard University Graduate School of Education have produced a series of publications that distinguish, among forms of integrity, an ethic of care from an ethic of justice. This research suggests that the typical patriarchal assumption that integrity resides in an elaborated system of justice does not speak to the experience of those who are motivated by an ethic of care. Gilligan notes that this assumption has particularly skewed the evaluation of women's moral development.

Women often relate their integrity more to an ethic of care than to an ethic of justice. Immanuel Kant, for instance, seems to have believed one should never tell a lie, even if a life were at stake: the life of the principle of truth was more important to him.[17] This is a view few women would hold, according to Gilligan's research.[18] We can see in Gilligan's formulation, which has been so helpful in teaching us to read women's narratives for what they say about their style of integrity, a vision of two styles of moral consciousness that ultimately derives from

Jung. Jung gives the styles that Gilligan calls "care" and "justice" the names *eros* and *logos*.

Eros is a somewhat unfortunate term. Jung used the name of a male god to convey the feminine principle of moral understanding. It would help to follow Gilligan in realizing that eros is a moral attitude. By eros Jung means neither sex nor relatedness in any casual sense, but rather the need to cultivate caring for the wholeness of others as well as of oneself. Jung's eros is not unlike Austen's amiability, and it is part of a conception of integrity that he does not explicitly define. To borrow the language of Taoist philosophy, eros would be the *te* that senses a feminine Tao.

Logos, in contrast, means the capacity to differentiate and discriminate, implying a conception of justice by which such discriminations can be made. Justice differs from caring and wholeness in being something obtained from the father, the way our Founding Fathers gave us the Constitution, and it is often conceived as something to be passed on to a son, like Polonius's advice, and Cicero's.

Such advice is not the psychoanalytic way. Even Freud, for all his emphasis on the father, and what Jacques Lacan has argued is an implicit morality of the "word" and the patriarchal "symbolic order," established a matriarchal ethic for psychotherapy. This matriarchal value was put in place with his basic rule that the patient should say anything that came to mind, that the associations should be free, and the thinking undirected by the analyst. The rule implied from the start that there is a pre-existing integrity to mental process that psychological healing taps. Freud's image of the wise psychotherapist, just as much as Jung's, was one who agreed to let nature take its course, a matriarchal attitude.

Jung had the bad taste to make this premise explicit, and

it cost him his place at the psychoanalytic table. It was he who upset Freud's project of creating a depth psychology that Western medicine could accept, by revealing how radically far from the patriarchal base of that medicine psychoanalysis was likely to go. His demonstration of the matriarchal thrust of analysis came in a book that Freud finally could not accept, *Wandlungen und Symbole der Libido,* a study of a patient's fantasies around the mother image.[19] There Jung implied that regression to the mother was not only a movement of the psyche in the disturbed patient but also a need of our culture that psychoanalysis was perfectly suited to meet. The conclusion was that, however patriarchal its language sounded, psychoanalysis was finally matriarchal in its aims: Freud had created the basis for a creative return by modern consciousness from the directed thinking of the Father back into the spontaneous flow of ideas that originates in the Mother.[20] These spontaneous ideas would be the seeds of a new, future consciousness, and Jung saw analysis as going along with the regression because it afforded the possibilities of personal and cultural renewal.[21]

Today, this idea does not sound so odd to us; we know, or at least are fond of believing, that analysis has become a precinct of the Goddess, with her religion of feelings, visions, empathy, and the body, and creative descents to deeper levels of the psyche. We feel analysis to be a ritual belonging to a broader psychological attitude that touches all people in the West today, whether they have had a formal psychotherapy or not, one that involves a serious new acceptance of the feminine. But Freud was hardly ready for this idea in 1912, and he certainly was not willing to admit that he had arranged the marriage of the ambitious new science of psychoanalysis to the socially disreputable Great Mother, with her "black tide" of occult relatives.[22] Freud attempted, with considerable temporary success, to get the developing field of depth psychology to blind itself, like a new Oedipus, to what Jung would otherwise have made it see, the Mother's body in the mess of mythological thinking psychoanalysis had released.

Only recently has depth psychology been willing to follow Jung in recognizing the potential order that resides in this apparent chaos of the Mother. Our sense of the integrity of the Mother has awaited a scientific perspective, now at hand in the newest Western scientific craze, chaos theory, as well as in the ongoing revival of Taoist philosophical ideas. It is not hard to point to Jung's role in creating the psychological receptivity to this kind of thinking, but we may have forgotten his original insight, in *Wandlungen und Symbole der Libido,* that, as the creative unconscious, the Chaotic Mother has a purposiveness unique to herself in supporting the growth of personality.

In later years, Jung would sometimes accept the matriarchal fantasy of growth uncritically, as when he tried to stop Emma Jung from ever cutting back plants in their Zurich garden, feeling that things should just be allowed to grow as they would—evidence, perhaps, that Jung had, personally, a fairly strong positive mother complex.[23] And *Wandlungen und Symbole der Libido,* so far as we can reconstruct it in English through the translation of Beatrice Hinkle of 1916 and the ponderous extensive revision Jung brought out in 1954, was not only *about* a mother complex; it reads as if it were written by a mother complex. It shows off, it does not know when to stop, its argument turns on itself, and almost all the trace of masculine purpose it claims to discover seems drenched, if not drowned, in the sea of unconscious material that belongs to its wild journey through the night sea. Often Jung leaves us unsure as to how to feel about the material he dredges up, a sure sign that a masculine capacity for evaluation has not yet emancipated itself from the mother that is being explored.

This was not the last of Jung's books to display this regressive rhetorical tendency, although it is the only one to be followed by such a severe regression in Jung himself. The "creative illness" of 1913–19 signified Jung's personal willingness to return to the Mother as the basis of his psychology, and it left traces of the matriarchal in many places in his work—in the excessively positive value he places upon the unconscious, in his interest in health and growth, and in his unqualified acceptance of synchronicity. This matriarchal thinking, however appealingly argued, can seem to a hard-nosed patriarchal science to be inspirational at best, and at worst loosely mystical and credulously magical.

What is less obvious, perhaps, is the achievement of Jung in constructing for himself an essentially healthy matriarchal psychology. Jung's own mother had not been this whole. In his autobiography, *Memories, Dreams, Reflections,* Jung tells us:

> She held all the conventional opinions a person was obliged to have, but then her unconscious personality would suddenly put in an appearance. That personality was unexpectedly powerful: a somber, imposing figure possessed of unassailable authority—and no bones about it. I was sure that she consisted of two personalities, one innocuous and human, the other uncanny. This other emerged only now and then, but each time it was unexpected and frightening. She would then speak as if talking to herself, but what she said was aimed at me and usually struck to the core of my being, so that I was stunned into silence. . . .
>
> There was an enormous difference between my mother's two personalities. That was why as a child I often had anxiety dreams about her. By day she was a loving mother, but at night she seemed uncanny. Then she was like one of those seers who is at the same time a strange animal, like a priestess in a bear's cave. Archaic and ruthless; ruthless as truth and nature. At such moments she was the embodiment of what I have called the "natural mind."[24]

As Jung makes clear, "this quality never properly emerged; it remained hidden beneath the semblance of a kindly, fat old woman, extremely hospitable, and possessor of a great sense of humor."[25] Therefore the two sides of his mother's personality took on the character of an inner split rather than facets of an integrated whole, and one senses that the young Jung found this lack of integration in her, and in his image of her, deeply upsetting. Further, there was a painful separation from his mother around the age of two and a half or three.

> I was suffering, so my mother told me afterward, from general eczema. Dim intimations of trouble in my parents' marriage hovered around me. My illness, in 1878, must have been connected with a temporary separation of my parents. My mother spent several months in a hospital in Basel, and presumably her illness had something to do with the difficulty in the marriage. An aunt of mine, who was a spinster and some twenty years older than my mother, took care of me. I was deeply troubled by my mother's being away. From then on, I always felt mistrustful when the word "love" was spoken. The feeling I associated with "woman" was for a long time that of innate unreliability. "Father," on the other hand, meant reliability and—powerlessness. That is the handicap I started off with.[26]

In a psychoanalytic essay, "At the Mercy of Another: Abandonment and Restitution in Psychosis and Psychotic Character," Jeffrey Satinover has put forward the view that Jung's extraordinary creativity does not obscure an underlying psychopathology. He presents Jung as someone who had to compensate all his life for an early lack of maternal security. Later rejections, significantly the one by Freud, reawakened the original sense of abandonment and persecution at the hands of his mother, as well as the lack of protection by his father, and Jung was forced to defend himself by elaborating a set of matriarchal ideas within which he was able to contain his otherwise overwhelming emotions.

One way to look at the archetypes, for instance, is as image-personifications of affects that would otherwise have been lost to Jung through dissociation to avoid their pain, and as inner fantasy figures to make up for the impoverishment of an internal object world. Satinover contends that there was insufficient internalization of human objects, a condition which a working-through of the ambivalence associated with his mother's abandonments might have corrected. Personified archetypal figures substituted, in this view, for real internal objects; the archetypes both expressed the emotions that arose out of a profound experience of abandonment and substituted for the lost objects.[27]

From this perspective, the relative gender rigidity of some of Jung's conceptualizations betrays a somewhat schizoid inner core. Yet such relatively rigid formulations also enabled Jung to achieve a dramatic realization of unconscious dynamics. By means of a clarifying binary scheme involving pairs of gender opposites — logos/eros, anima/animus, sol/luna, masculine/feminine — he was able to discriminate moral positions within psychology more sharply than anyone else had done. This allowed Jung, like Jane Austen, to go beyond patriarchal definitions of integrity — beyond the justice tradition that had prevailed since Cicero, and beyond the conscience tradition that his own Swiss Protestantism might have convinced him was sufficient.

The Man in the Moon

Jung was to formulate for psychology a feminine image of the integrity of personality, appropriately carried by his feminine name for personality, psyche. This construction may well have begun in his efforts to create a secure, whole mother image for himself, attempting within his own depths to resolve the contraries in his mother's character. However, the project led him beyond the mother, which in his psychology finally remained a dual image — a positive mother and a negative mother — to the discovery of a truly integrated feminine figure — the anima — capable of consistent development over the course of a lifetime. In this work, first on the dynamics of the dual mother, and then on the anima's role in supporting the unification of personality, Jung found a system of integrity well beyond anything Western culture had previously imagined. It is probably inevitable that depth psychological schools should enfold upon themselves to analyze their founders, so that the current debates within analytical psychology over the actual level of integration this great pioneer achieved are not surprising. I do not propose to resolve them here, but rather to point out the role Jung's early and later disintegrative experiences had in leading him to uncover this unsuspected layer of potential integrity.

Finding the anima was for Jung like finding the possibility of having an Anne Elliot within, to manage the chaotic world of internal object relations in a conscious and coordinated way. Jung often spoke of the anima as his bridge to the Self, and I think we must recognize that this also meant that the Self, for him, despite its formal definition as a union of opposites, male and female, had the essential characteristic of receptive sensitivity, which for Jung was feminine. In fact, Jung implies strongly in one place that we never quite get to the Self, but rather develop our receptivity to this unknowable, but all-important center of personality:

> Sensing the [S]elf as something irrational, as an indefinable existent, to which the ego is neither opposed nor subjected, but merely attached, and about which it revolves very much as the earth revolves round the sun — thus we come to the goal of individuation. I use the word "sensing" in order to indicate the apperceptive character of the relation between ego and [S]elf.[28]

Jung seems to have believed that such "sensing" emerged as he integrated the anima. His image of sensitized psychological awareness is not unlike Austen's portrayal of the consciousness of a constant woman. Jung's source for the idea of the constant receptivity of the anima, however, would have been Chinese philosophy, where a gendered notion of integrity has a long tradition. In the Taoist-Confucian *I Ching*, for instance, which was well-known to Jung from 1919 on, the second hexagram, K'un, called in the Wilhelm translation Jung used "The Receptive," is composed all of "yin" lines, that is, lines with a hole in the middle. According to Confucian tradition, this hexagram is associated with the female-maternal and is seen as the opposite number to the male-paternal hexagram "The Creative," which is made up of straight, unbroken "yang" lines.

The distinction between being and doing could hardly be more clear than this association of yin with receiving and yang with creating. This feminine hexagram is associated, like so many feminine deities in the West, and like women themselves in many traditions, with the earth. (The all-yang hexagram, like the masculine sky gods in many parts of the world, is associated with Heaven.) But beyond this careful delimitation of the scope of the feminine, there is a startling association of this hexagram of feminine receptivity with the Tao itself, an association with great implications for our understanding of the ground of integrity. The ruling line of the K'un hexagram reads:

> Straight, square, great.
> Without purpose,
> Yet nothing remains unfurthered.

Richard Wilhelm comments: "Nature creates all beings without erring: this is its straightness. It is calm and still: this is its foursquareness. It tolerates all creatures equally: this is its greatness. Therefore it attains what is right for all without artifice or special intentions. Man achieves the height of wisdom when all that he does is as self-evident as what nature does."[29]

This is of course an essential Taoist idea, developed in Chapter 25 of the *Tao Te Ching:*

> Man patterns himself on earth,
> Earth patterns itself on heaven,
> Heaven patterns itself on Tao;
> And Tao is spontaneously patterned of itself [tao chih tzu-jan].[30]

A commentator on this passage has noted that:

> One of the most characteristic descriptions of the "life" of the Tao is that it is completely self-generated and returning in on itself, going out and coming back in a completely spontaneous and creative way. Its basic rule and pattern of life is its utter self-contained freedom of movement, its *tzu-jan,* which constitutes in Taoism one of the most important technical terms for the perfect freedom of pure spontaneity and naturalness attained through an identification with Tao. To be *tzu-jan* is to have the wholeness and freedom that was present at the beginning, to be completely "self-so" in that all actions and thoughts are generated internally and spontaneously in harmony with the organic law of cosmic life itself.[31]

This image of integrity is built around an identification with the primordial naturalness of the Mother, one of whose symbols is the empty center found throughout the lines of the second hexagram of the *I Ching.* This is more than a gross anatomical reference to the female body. "It is the empty gap of the center that allows for the original movement, sound, or flow of the life-principle."[32]

Psychotherapists have been exceptionally concerned to protect this free circulation of libido. It is the point of the chaste framework of therapy—Winnicott's holding environment and Jung's *vas bene clausum,* the well-sealed alchemical container—to make a safe space through which the freest expression of feeling can flow, which is then allowed to do its own work of taking the patient's psyche where it needs to go. All this is in the service of a feminine conception of integrity that we can trace to Jung's first intimation of regression to the mother as healing and that in his later work Jung associates with the Virgin archetype of the Middle Ages, an image of grace and safety that encompasses both mother and anima.[33]

What psychotherapists have less known how to adapt to their own practices is Jung's way of using words, which he did not hesitate to deploy with telling decisiveness. According to the published reports of people who saw him for analysis,[34] Jung talked continually—gave advice, criticized, explained, lectured, questioned, confronted, self-revealed, read aloud, and even sang[35] to his patients—did not, in short, hesitate to use the full range of verbal interventions at his disposal in the effort to heal. This is, I think, where Jung's masculinity most often surfaced in treatment, and it is perhaps not accidental that he called the masculine principle the *logos* principle, nor surprising that for this part of our understanding of Jung's idea of integrity we have to rely on an oral tradition. That tradition has it that Jung was good at saying the thing that shouldn't be said—as to the pretentious man with a ridiculous ascot tie, who heard at the end of his first hour with Jung, "And take that tie off. It does nothing for you!"[36]

For Jung, the masculine was a position taken towards the unconscious, a standpoint (and to this image we can associate the bodily image of "uprightness" that we have seen is an archetypal, and I think masculine, representation of integrity). In an active imagination, it was not enough to have just a receptive experience of the fantasy. If a bear appeared, you did something. "What was your reaction?" would be the first question he addressed to anyone's account of an archetypal image.

The problem with the picture of Jung created by the oral tradition is less his insistence on active participation in the treatment — there is much in this that contemporary psychotherapy might learn from — than on the sense we get of that participation being so aggressive. It is tempting to offer explanations that refer to Jung's ethnic background (Germanic), his astrological character (Leo), his psychoanalytic personality structure (phallic narcissistic), and especially to his magnitude (genius of the psychological attitude), but none of these speak to what I think is a limitation in Jung's integrity on the masculine side. One way I recognize this limitation is by the near complete absence of any sense of inhibiting shame in Jung's accounts of the way he deals with his patients. This is not the shamelessness of sociopathy, because Jung is not at all afraid to be wrong, and to tell his patients that he has been wrong. It is just that he doesn't seem to have any anxiety telling a patient one of his own dreams, making a critical remark, using his authority in the transference.

Perhaps there is something one-sided about Jung's masculinity. We can see a limitation of Jung's own integration in his late formulation of *sol* and *luna* as the masculine and feminine principles. To draw upon a recent formulation by Howard Teich, Jung's masculinity, both in his theory and in his personality, seems too one-sidedly *solar*. Teich has proposed that we should see solar and lunar not as metaphors for the two genders, but as dimensions that modify gender, appearing as polarities within both masculinity and femininity. Rather than conflating masculine with solar, he has adduced clinical evidence to suggest that a whole masculinity will consist of both solar and lunar parts. By solar he means active and aggressive and by lunar receptive and responsive. These parts appear alongside each other in many

traditions as male twins. It is revealing of our patriarchal culture that Romulus, the solar twin, should have killed Remus,
the lunar twin, after the founding of Rome.[37] Teich feels that
there is also a twinship for women involving solar and lunar
femininity. In her poem "Integrity," Adrienne Rich calls this
pair "anger and tenderness, my selves."[38] Our most familiar examples of the attempt to reconcile these opposites come from
Hollywood movies, where, sometimes portrayed by the same
actress playing twins, sometimes by famous rivals, and increas-
ingly by apparent friends, the opposed natures reconcile their
differences. It is the eventual reconciliation of the two sides of
her nature that helps to make the individuation of Anne Elliot
so convincing.

It is just this sense of internal twinship, of a comfortable
tension between a solar masculinity that is aggressive and a lunar
masculinity that is receptive, that I miss in Jung. Indeed, as
Teich has pointed out, Jung seems to project his lunar masculinity onto women, seeing them as natural receivers or containers
— a projection we have already met in Marina Warner's sieve of
Tuccia. Teich's formulation validates and helps me to understand
a sense I have had that Jung had difficulty sustaining receptivity
to the ideas of other men; he could not relinquish control enough
to be more than illuminated by another man's solar energy.

My own belief is that Jung could not be penetrated by other
men's ideas because of very early fears of his own unusually strong
phallic potential, an anxiety compounded by experience of homosexual seduction by an older mentor when he was eighteen.[39]
Jung's childhood dream of a phallus on an underground throne
is well known, and I need only quote from the central part of
it here:

> It was a magnificent throne, a real king's throne in a fairy
> tale. Something was standing on it which I thought at first

was a tree trunk twelve to fifteen feet high and about one and a half to two feet thick. It was a huge thing, reaching almost to the ceiling. But it was of a curious composition: it was made of skin and naked flesh, and on top there was something like a rounded head with no face and no hair. On the very top of the head was a single eye, gazing motionlessly upward.

It was fairly light in the room, although there were no windows and no apparent source of light. Above the head, however, was an aura of brightness. The thing did not move, yet I had the feeling that it might at any moment crawl off the throne like a worm and creep toward me. I was paralyzed with terror. At that moment, I heard from outside and above me my mother's voice. She called out, "Yes, just look at him. That is the man eater!"[40]

The homosexual anxiety is obvious, as is the mother's role in intensifying the panic. We need to look beyond this screen of homosexual panic to find the moral *telos* in the anxiety. I regard the fear within this dream as compensatory to the lack of fear that Jung tended to show in displaying the phallic side of himself—his creativity, his exhibitionism, and his masculine authority, all of which were in abundant evidence throughout his life. Though underground, and Hermetic, the phallos here looks upward with its only eye in a solar direction, and "above the head" is "an aura of brightness," further developing the solar association.[41]

A purpose of the dream is to get Jung to fear the monocular vision associated with such a perspective. Following Teich's model, the fear would belong to this grandiose masculinity's missing twin, the more reflective side of Jung, his "lunar masculinity," which might rather look down than up, as it recalls an earlier, more matriarchal, stage of development. The terror belongs to a part of the little boy that had reason to fear the emerging phallic ambition of the budding genius. Enormous creativity was of course the Tao of Jung's nature, but the *te*, the integrity, lay in the boy's anxiety that this creativity would step beyond its rightful place and threaten the rest of Jung's nature. It is precisely this anxiety which is not reported in some of the mature Jung's displays of insight; it's as if he is fearless, and out of balance, in these accounts.

Jung of course achieved the promise of the Hermetic creativity revealed to him in this dream; with his extraordinary intuition, he became the most penetrating analyst of the unconscious that we have had, but as Teich's helpful formulation lets us see more clearly, something got left behind, with detrimental effect not just to Jung's relation to Freud, in which he felt himself called so often to yield, and to his relation to patients, with whom it was difficult for him not to take the lead, but in his relation to the archetypes of gender themselves. As Teich tells us:

> In Jungian thought, the moon-man is often confused with the anima. Jung built his psychology on the central female-male configuration of anima/animus, equating the moon (Luna) with the anima, or feminine, and labelling the Sun (Sol) as animus, or masculine. These gender labels assigned Sol to the unconscious "masculine side" (animus) in women. Similarly, lunar energies in men were tied to their unconscious "feminine side" (anima), making it clear to men that lunar behaviors belonged to the feminine.
> But if we dig deep enough in the mythologies of virtually any culture — including our own — we find that at some point the "sun-man" was almost always born with a "lunar" twin.[42]

I believe that sometimes Jung owned the receptivity of his own lunar masculinity, but often the anima, or a woman carrying the projection of his anima, was forced to bear an anxious receptivity he could not realize as part of himself. In his model of relationship, woman is the container, man the contained: he projected his own containing side onto Toni Wolff, who would be flooded with his unacknowledged affects, and onto Emma Jung, who would have to tolerate his rages. Everyone feels a rigidity in Jung's understanding of gender opposites. A reason Teich offers is that the masculine and feminine principles are not given their chance to develop polarities within themselves before they are asked to meet each other.

I think we would do well by integrity to take up Teich's suggestion; solar and lunar opposites exist within each gender and naturally hold each other's excesses in check, in the healthy regulation of the gender opposites. We might begin to move past homosexual panic in the way we relate to ourselves, recognizing lunar masculinity and solar femininity not as effeminacy or mannishness, but as complements to the solar masculinity and lunar femininity that Western patriarchy has emphasized. Instead of training men to grow past their lunar masculinity and women to suppress their solar femininity in deference to men, we might help men balance solar and lunar masculinity, and women lunar and solar femininity, in the conscious leading of their lives.

These considerations should make us look more carefully at Jung's conception of the union of male and female opposites as wholeness. As we have seen, wholeness within Jung's psychology, like previous notions of integrity within our patriarchal culture—virginity, chastity, and constancy—has had a feminine cast. Under the seductive spell of the anima, Jung's master concept, we have accepted this femininity as belonging to the territory, as Chinese philosophy would have us accept the Tao as somehow feminine, even though it unites the opposites of male and female too. Perhaps we should be more wary of the patriarchal anima. There is still a recollecting of projection to be

done before we can understand integrity within a gendered conception. The wholeness Jung sought initially through the mother
archetype, and later through the anima, denies the split within
his own masculine nature, a split that I think he was finally
too proud to recognize.

Today we are able to see the effects of this split as a partial
failure of integrity, obvious in his personal and political dealings with other men as well as in what he asked women to
carry for him. As Teich implies, Jung's failure to see the danger
of not resolving first the opposites within the gender to which
one belongs compromises his claim to understanding the integrity of personality as the *coniunctio* of developed gender principles.[43] The moral consequences of any dissociation of either
lunar or solar elements of personality are serious, for as Murray
Stein was able to point out nearly twenty years ago, there is
"a polarity in conscience" between "solar and lunar aspects."[44]

As Stein demonstrated, patriarchal Western civilization is
used to imagining these two styles of conscience sitting down
together as father and mother debating how to discipline the
children, and Jung's idea of the *coniunctio* has made this parental
colloquy into a conversation which we should all strive to achieve
within. But if we are to realize an ideal of integrity that is appropriate to a post-patriarchal age, the masculine and feminine
principles must each be allowed to become less monolithic by
developing the dialogue of solar and lunar conscience within
each principle. The gender principles need to find the opposites
within themselves before they turn to meet each other.

In demonstrating how the feminine principle develops itself before it attempts to meet the masculine, Jane Austen's image of constancy is a quiet beacon of the kind of integrity required to prepare for the *coniunctio*. Her best female characters
reflect a subtle unification of patience and force that makes one

suspect that she herself had resolved the lunar and solar possibilities of her own feminine nature. Because the union of sames is the project that must precede the union of opposites for individuation to have a convincing texture, Austen's contribution remains on the leading edge of integrity. Nevertheless, Jung's image of a final union between developed gender opposites is our culture's strongest vision of moral wholeness.

Like Austen, whose female characters seem far more integrated than her male ones, who mainly command with their manners, Jung seems to have achieved in his own opus a femininity that combined both solar and lunar aspects, aspects, that is, of brilliant outspokenness and quiet reflection in the service of the total personality. And like Austen, he could not come up with a masculine character that was truly equal to the challenge of relating to an integrated femininity: he had to settle for a brilliant masculine persona.

That two geniuses of this rank would stumble in the same way should disturb us: it appears that in our culture the anxieties attendant upon uniting male opposites are greater than those associated with the uniting of female opposites. We have assumed too long that this is a homosexual anxiety, greater in men than in women. It is really a moral anxiety, reflecting a failure on the part of solar masculinity to accept a brake on itself, and a failure on the part of lunar masculinity to honor its fear of solar masculinity by any other means than projection of that fear onto women. This is the anxiety that was beginning to surface in Jung's childhood dream. That Jung could be made to feel fear of solar masculinity was an early sign that the men of our age are ready to withdraw the projection of their vulnerability. But though Jung saw more clearly than anyone else the need to include the feminine within the patriarchal standpoint, he stopped short of a real confrontation between solar masculinity and the rest of his masculine nature. He did however leave his unresolved childhood dream in his autobiography as part of his psychological legacy.

Men should take up this problem, not as so many think now, by activating the unclaimed portion of their solar potential that may still lie underground,[45] but by allowing their very fear of that part of themselves to be their sign that another aspect of their maleness is in danger of violation. They should not rush Jung's goal of uniting genders within. The anima will wait for them to complete this preliminary work of meeting their phallic power with appropriate vulnerability. The anima, and also women. As Jane Austen's work signals, women have long been ready to unite the opposites within their gender. It is time for men to prepare to meet them with a similar integrity.

4.

Working on Integrity

FIDELITY TO PROCESS

IT HAS ALWAYS STRUCK COMMENTATORS as paradoxical that, in the midst of his greatest play about the difficulty of restoring integrity, Shakespeare should have put the words that speak most directly to his theme into the mouth of Polonius:

> First above all: to thine own self be true,
> And it must follow, as the night the day,
> Thou canst not then be false to any man.

"A scheming old windbag exhorts his headstrong son to be true to himself—to be constant and self-consistent,"[1] complains Willeford, while Trilling concedes that "our impulse to make its sense consistent with our general view of Polonius is defeated by the way the lines sound, by their lucid moral lyricism."[2]

Something like this ambivalent reaction pursues anyone who tries to tell another that integrity is important. It creates the reservations we feel about taking similar advice from Cicero, whose *De Officiis* seems to be parodied in the rest of Polonius's speech; and we resent it eventually, too, from Milton, for all his sincerity. This may be why the field of depth psychology has been slow to accept hectoring from its parent figures that integrity is crucial to mental health. In the late 1960s and early

1970s, while O. Hobart Mowrer was advocating an "integrity therapy,"[3] Karl Menninger put forward concerns about ethics, asking "Whatever became of sin?"[4] The field heard Polonius's voice and found it hard to metabolize the message. Leo Rangell's call, after Watergate, for an examination by psychoanalysts of "the syndrome of compromise of integrity,"[5] likewise went almost completely unheeded. Despite the much greater interest today in the ethical dimension of therapy, formulations of this dimension continue to suffer from the advising tone of Polonius, whose mode of moral imperative is adopted in the title of one of the better recent books, *To Thine Own Self Be True.*[6]

A first step, then, in working with integrity is to work through our ambivalence about being advised to do so. If we are really to make integrity part of depth psychology, and therefore an issue for the therapist and patient in depth work, we have to take the notion of integrity out of the realm of collective counsel, which supports a false self of superego expectations.

Here the dramatic action of *Hamlet* can serve as a guide to the process a patient may have to follow. If we look to the way the advising Polonius functions in *Hamlet,* we can see that he belongs, as a character, to the wider dramatic structure of the kingdom of falsity that the prince must find a way to tear down. In the analogy to individual personality, this structure would refer to the inauthentic persona that in analytic work is referred to as the false self. Claudius's corrupt kingdom represents a false-father world that Hamlet must destroy to assert the principles of the true father. Before it is over, Hamlet will have killed, or led to kill themselves, Claudius, Gertrude, Polonius, and Polonius's two children, Ophelia and Laertes. All these characters belong to the world of the pseudo-father or mother's animus, a stage of object relations that is, from the developmental standpoint, prior to the emergence of the true father stage. The murder of Hamlet's father by his mother's animus is a psychological regression from the higher level of development. It represents a compromise of integrity for which, in this Orestean drama, the mother must be punished, along with her animus entourage. Their sin lies in repressing the moral consciousness that the father represents.

The ghost of Hamlet's father beckons to the prince like a stage of psychological development that has been cheated, and it is all Hamlet can do to be a hero worthy of him by returning the realm of Denmark to a patriarchal state. For most of the play, he is mainly a resentful trickster railing at his complacent mother for her support of false-father values. These are values that Jungian psychology associates with the negative mother's animus — haste, double-dealing, emphasis upon a collective persona, and expediency — and their effect on a son or daughter is to paralyze the initiative required to achieve a genuine integrity in one's dealings with the world, though the mother continues to expect such integrity. Polonius advising Laertes is like an animus advising a child to observe integrity when the actual parent does not. Psychologically Polonius is an animus extension of the mother, and it is dramatically right that Polonius be killed by Hamlet when Gertrude fears that her son is about to murder her.[7] From the standpoint of moral development, Polonius is the image of the patriarchal animus, whose rigid demand for the appearance of integrity is the enemy of true integrity in depth.

Persona integrity — that mask for the ambition to respectability which serves to make the status quo look more attractive — is what, in a culture dominated by the patriarchal animus, we eventually all suspect in the advice of our parents — in the advice of our most developed cultural forebears, Cicero, the moral philosophers, Milton, and even at times in the maddening clarity of Jane Austen. There is a stage when we feel ruled by the good advice of our parents, and by collective wisdom.

When such integrity has grown rigid and inauthentic in the
course of advancing psychological and moral development, we
may have to kill it off as suddenly as Hamlet kills Polonius,
in order to move on to an integrity that is more adequate to
the stage the psyche is attempting to reach. The higher level
of integrity requires a passion that breaks free of the dampening
effect of the patriarchal animus; this passion partakes of the anima
that appears only at the truly fatherly stage of development to
support moral initiative. Erich Neumann and Joseph Henderson have made clear the stages by which consciousness proceeds
in both sexes to an openness to the father in which the anima
can be realized.[8] James Hillman insists that we must consider
the anima a prerogative of both sexes, something the patriarchal animus psychology that we call, in political discourse, "patriarchy" has tried to deny.[9] At first this anima is an attribute
of the loved and idealized father, but gradually it is internalized
as the emotional conviction of the developing daughter or son.
It is the failure of his mother Gertrude to be his father's anima
that occasions Hamlet's rage. This resentment is a narcissistic
fury over his inability to find an ideal part of the parent with
which his developing energy can merge to consolidate the initiative he needs to complete his moral purpose. Yet this very
rage contains the anima he needs, the life force for psychological movement.

Work with patients continually impresses a therapist with
the need to respect rage as a vehicle of integrity. Even in very
longstanding relationships characterized by a good working
alliance, rage may sometimes surface to affirm the self more
strongly than the therapy has allowed. Recently, a long-term
patient of mine began to chafe in her sessions at a tendency
I have to make her feel the way her mother used to when they
would talk about her feelings. Although she has often brought

this impression to my attention in recent months, it was hard for her until quite recently to get across to me exactly what I have been doing to upset her. This central discomfort in the transference has been disconcerting to both of us, because she has been seeing me for many years, with considerable clarification of other areas of her life. It is particularly upsetting because we are both committed to our work together and do not want to terminate it without resolving the awkwardness. My patient has brought me many dreams, shared her life situation in full with me, and knows much about me as a person and as a psychotherapist. I believe we are honest with each other and mutually committed to facing any truth together, however unpleasant.

The other day she described two telephone calls of great significance to her current life situation, and how she had decided to handle both. I was careful to listen and not to intrude with advice, which I've worried can be preemptive of her own ability to deal with the situation, which is complex and does engage my supportive concern. Then she reported a dream to me, in which she described making a difficult turn in the road without overturning her car. Sensing that this dream referred to her handling of the first call, I commented, "Well you did make the difficult turn in the call."

"Which call?" she responded in a loud, irritated voice that sounded to my ears full of contempt for me.

"Don't you remember?" I said, pointing out that she had just finished telling me about how she had handled a tricky obstacle in communication in one of the calls. She reminded me that there had been two calls, then proceeded to tell me that it bothered her that I had been so quick to come back at her: I had been "right in there" with my "Don't you remember?" as if to deny her right to be upset when confused by me.

I said that I knew I had been aggressive, and that I thought it was in response to the withering tone in her voice in asking me "which call."

"Well, so what?" was her response. "You were wrong. I can't be expected to damp down my instinctive response. That's all a person has."

I still thought to myself that she was not according me any more room to breathe than I had accorded her in defending myself: I had been more incomplete than wrong in referring to "the call" when trying to define the turn in the road signified by the dream. I censored my wish to debate with her. I worried that leaving my full reaction out might lack integrity, but overrode this consideration in favor of the deeper sense I was getting that her anger at how I had reacted to her touchiness was what we needed to follow now. I decided to let it have power over me by sticking with it rather than insisting on my feelings, a decision that made me intensely anxious but seemed somehow correct. (To use Teich's formulation, I had to enter a lunar masculine mode to reflect and not compete with the sudden clarity of her emerging solar femininity.)

"You're telling me that you're getting a message from me to tone it down."

"Yes," she said, recalling that she had felt this message before. She remembered a look on my face from a few months back when she was angry and confused. She got the feeling that I didn't want her to be angry then, that it wasn't okay to be upset. Again I felt the literal unfairness of this assertion, since I have been devoted throughout our work to the recognition of her feelings. Nevertheless, I continued to listen to the point she was trying to make. She reminded me that as the therapist I "carry weight" and that it was especially important for her that she not be turned against her instinctive responses since she had been taught to distrust them at such an early age.

"I guess this does remind you of your mother," I said.

"Does it go back to her?" she asked, in a disappointed tone.

I realized that I had deflected and diminished her challenge by taking the opportunity to put the problem in the past. This was between us.

"This is happening now," I said; "I'm your mother now." I heard a consultant's voice within saying, "Shouldn't you say, 'It's *as if* I am your mother now'?" but disregarded it. In this moment I was her mother, whether I wanted to be or not. And suddenly I wanted to be, even though my willingness to foster her feeling didn't soften the force of her anger.

She mentioned suddenly that she was a feeling person. We realized almost immediately that this was the key to her psychological type, a discrimination we had never been able to make to our mutual satisfaction. Insights about our process seemed to tumble out in a rush. It became obvious to me that my patient was an introverted feeling type, and I quickly relayed my thought that her thinking would move more slowly.

"That sounds like me!" she rejoined. "I'm not at all unintelligent, but a slow thinker," she said. Planning her life had been difficult, and a job that had required her to keep up with a highly verbal boss had undermined her self-confidence. Now we could see that this was because her extraverted thinking had not been fast-paced enough.

It was now painfully obvious why my inexact remark had upset her so: my casual choice of words had not only threatened the feeling foundation of her relation to reality by seeming to foist a wrong interpretation on her, but had also confused her in the place where she is most vulnerable to confusion, the area of personality that Jung has called "the inferior function," which in her case is thinking.[10] My patient's rude tone in saying with such obvious irritation "Which call?" had what von Franz, in her classic presentation of this region of character, has described as "the barbaric quality of the inferior function."[11]

I believe with von Franz that access to the deep integrity of personality can be gained only through this primitive inferior function, and by a person who is well grounded in the standpoint of the superior function. I had assumed that I had established this conscious orientation long ago with my patient, although a chronic failure to make her personal authority prevail in the world might have led me to question this assumption. I had reasoned that her problem with the world was a consequence of inferior extraverted sensation, that is, having in short supply the function that manages practically in the world. For years in the therapy we had said that she was an introverted intuitive type. However, more recently she had begun to tell me that Jung's type theory didn't make as much sense to her as the alternative formulation for women that Toni Wolff had put forward. Wolff's was a typology of structural forms; she postulated that women, being more holistic than men, would tend to organize their identities around their roles, which most often were mother, amazon, medium, and sexual comrade. My patient, who is uncannily good at sensing things about other people, had decided that she was a medial woman. Now she could see that she was an introverted feeling type as well, and suddenly Jung's type theory made more sense for her. I think it is important to point out that according to Jung and von Franz, the inferior function in a woman is carried by the animus or masculine side,[12] and that this woman could begin to accept the typological ideas of a man only when I had allowed myself to accept the man in her unconscious.[13]

A subsequent session clarified that extraverted intuition was my patient's auxiliary function, and though it had not been exactly false to say that she was intuitive, doing so had denied the basic "spine" of her personality, which consists of a superior feeling connected to an inferior thinking. I had supposed some of the strain in our relationship to be based on her being an introverted intuitive while I was an extraverted intuitive. Instead it had been rooted in her being a rational type when I am an irrational type and had been increased by my near-complete obliviousness to the fact that thinking is much slower for her than it is for me. The inferior extraverted thinking, which carried her relation to the unconscious, had finally asserted itself to confront my more polite, fatherly, but sometimes best-understood-by-myself introverted thinking, the auxiliary function that I would employ in trying to define the images of her dreams. With her insistence on her right to be herself in impolitely asserting that her inferior extraverted thinking was confused, she dropped the anchor of her ego-Self axis and was able to assert her true feeling nature as the topsail of her ship.

Later she said, "It was like a miracle," and indeed it was. What had righted itself was her entire ego-Self axis, the "spine" of her personality. Real integrity ultimately depends upon the claiming of this spine in each of us; it is the inner basis of the "uprightness" we look for in ourselves and in each other. In my patient, introverted feeling is at the head, and extraverted thinking at the tail, of that spine; together they define the basis of her selfhood as a person.

It was essential that she defend her position of outrage at my failure to appreciate her right to get upset when she thought my interpretation was about to go wrong; her integrity was at stake. It required my integrity, particularly my capacity to accept shame, to see that I had indeed been like her mother in trying to get my patient to tone down the intensity of what was essentially her personality. One has to ask why such a difficult and subtle transaction is necessary to achieve the condition of integrity in the analytic relationship. I believe my patient gave the answer when she pointed out that her previous life experience had taught her to distrust herself. Hers is an example of a not uncommon central injury inflicted by the mother who cannot tolerate tension and the father who colludes by discouraging the child's discovery of intensity.

This intensity belongs to the archetype of life itself, the anima that Hillman feels is a prerogative of both sexes but in our culture has been particularly assigned to males. I feel that in seizing the initiative from me in defining her right to intensity my patient was claiming the anima in her therapy. I experienced this as a yielding of control to her which was difficult but important for the development of my own feeling. The effect on me has been to make me look at the way I deal with introverted feeling in myself, and to discover that despite previous work on this function, I habitually "tone it down" exactly as I was asking my patient to do.

At an appropriate moment in the session that initially led to these recognitions, I told her: "You've got me dead to rights. It's quite unconscious what I've been doing to you, but I do it to myself too. I think it's very important that you've brought this up." As I said this I realized that I had not only tried to damp down her intensity and my own, but that I had done so in a manipulative way. To admit as much I added, "I realize that I'm hard to confront." At this point we were working on *my* integrity.

By saying "Don't you remember?" as a way of speaking back to her angry feeling, as well as in temporarily deflecting the problem between us by shifting to her past difficulties with her mother, I had been warding off the transference rather than truly analyzing it. Giving up this manipulation was very hard to do; I felt I needed it to defend myself against unreasonable attack, and part of me was still angry to be made so wrong by her.

A dream soon after this session, however, showed me what I had gained by making room for her feeling with my own rather than retaliating in some controlling way. In the dream I had been given a wonderful new opportunity to work in a musical setting in a job that had been vacated by a conductor known for his great musical gifts but also for his manipulative handling of personal relations. A much quieter, more introverted friend of mine, also a composer and a man of great personal integrity, had long been working in this space, and at first I felt that this was his world. But now I was to work here too, as the musical director. It seemed inconceivable that I, who can barely read music, would be able to function effectively in a leading position, but the other musicians were friendly, and I realized that from now on conducting them would be my job. In the dream it made sense that with daily practice I would soon get used to the musical notation and grow fluent. I think the dream suggests that my work with my patient has initiated me into the possibility of my handling introverted feeling with much more integrity and competence.

THE PARADOXICAL DREAM

The special role of the dream in revealing the status of a dreamer's integrity is a hallmark of Jungian analysis. I have come to feel that monitoring integrity is one of the chief functions of the dream, and that it ought to guide the way we look at dreams and the way we work with them. I think I can make the contribution of Jungian analysis to the problem of integrity most clear if I give you an example of some work done with a dream from a man in his late forties.

At the time I saw him, I was also seeing his wife, who had been my initial patient. She was an unbelievably difficult patient, who would call me three times a day, seven days a week. If I didn't return her calls, she would call suicide prevention, whose policy was always to call the therapist, and she would be put through. For a time I had seen only her, then her with her husband as a couple, and finally each of them separately. He, like me (and many of their neighbors and friends), was making a heroic effort to contain her. In addition to his marital pressure, this man was under heavy stress at a job with an industrial firm, whose internal politics were continually frustrating his efforts to make a creative contribution.

Here is a dream he gave me near the end of his analytic work with me. It is in fact the dream which signalled his termination.

> Dream: It looked like a black [bottle] cap open side up—on its back—on the concrete pavement, sitting there all alone. I reached down to pick it up. The meaning was that "this is it."

In the notebook in which he had written this dream, which seemed on its face a bit absurd and probably unimportant to him, he had written "TRY GESTALT" and (following the method pioneered by Fritz Perls, to whose work he had been exposed) my patient jotted down some associations taken from the point of view of the dream object, the bottle cap itself. I read these associations to him and then had him read them back to me once, and then again. Here they are:

> I am a black cap sitting all alone on my back—receptive. I am both a cap to hold things in and keep the lid on or pressure in and a container to hold one measure, no more. I am molded from a monolithic shiny plastic material. I have somehow become separated from my container yet I am self-sufficient, a small hard vessel with enough structure and strength to hold in the contents of an entire bottle. *I can hold in far more than I can contain.* This is my life. I am the cap of the canteen, the cork, the stopper. I prevent contents from leaking, becoming lost or messy and wet. I am far stronger and harder than the bottle but also smaller and less

copious. If you will drink or partake you must first reckon with me. I am the watchdog at the gates — Cerberus. I keep a firm grip on the neck. Replace me when you have had your fill — I will continue to protect the rest!

When he had read these associations aloud the second time, I said, "But isn't that the role you've been playing on your job and in your marriage?"

It was a moment of self-recognition. The patient burst into tears and sobbed mightily for nearly ten minutes. This turned out to be the pivotal dream of his analysis. Within a month he had left his marriage and my practice, which had become identified with containing his marriage. (I referred him to an older, more experienced analyst.) Eventually he remarried happily and was able to leave his frustrating job for a much more satisfying line of work.

This is probably the most striking example I have personally witnessed of the transformative power of a single dream, and so it provided me a chance to see the healing power of dream work in an analytic setting in its complete range. As I have reflected on this work, I have come to see it in terms of three paradoxes that I think sum up the Jungian analytic approach to dreams. More generally, these paradoxes enable the therapy to include the unconscious in the effort to promote integrity. In making an intervention, a "move" toward interpreting a dream, I try to satisfy all three of these paradoxical conditions which the Jungian analytic tradition has set up for understanding and working with the dream.

Paradox one: The dream is alive, yet operates to bring an old attitude to its "death." That the dream is alive is of course at the heart of Jung's approach to the psyche. His notion of the living reality of the inner environment, the psyche, implies that the dream needs to be approached, like Yosemite, with an attitude of respect, with an ecological mindedness. We should backpack the dream, not strip mine it. We should be careful how we develop it. We can pollute it. I attempt to make my words about a dream exact, unintrusive, gentle in the sense that I roll with its own contours. If I have to be incisive, I am careful. I want to keep the dream alive. Yet, as James Hillman has pointed out, the dream, in its subtle way, serves death, not life: it takes an attitude out of the dayworld where it has been compulsively lived into the night, underworld, where it becomes a shade, an imaginal possibility, moved out of compulsive, living enactment.[14] Indeed in this dream the patient got for the first time an image of the role he was about to discard, that perhaps had already been discarded to the realm of psyche at the moment he had the dream. As he put it to me, in a letter written two years later,

> When I had the bottle cap dream and the realization which followed it, I felt for the first time I had made a model of myself. Looking back I think the change in me was instant just as the butterfly looks back at the chrysalis he has just broken out of. Today I no longer feel precious or small or lacking in content or holding capacity. I think the dream helped me . . . to realize it was time to stop strengthening and hardening and time to start containing, holding.

The second paradox of Jungian dream work concerns the therapeutic relationship in which the dream and the work on the dream happen. The dream registers the therapeutic relationship, making its unconscious aspect accessible to the understanding of both analyst and analysand, who may talk about it and work upon it. Yet it also is a picture of an objective, unconsciously structured transference/countertransference which is evolving, like an alchemical experiment, in ways that can only be observed, not controlled, by the conscious understanding of the partners. In this dream both the personal and the alchemical level of the analytic relationship are present. On the personal level, if the patient had been a bottle cap, compressing his life to hold in the tensions created by his wife and by his job, so, he now saw, was I. My life with her, and also my work, had become hell, as I took on an identification with his suffering which I mirrored to him. He saw his own self-denying compulsive codependency mirrored in me, and he chose to leave that role with me. On the deeper, alchemical level, where an analytic relationship is frequently symbolized by a container recalling the alchemical retort — the *vas bene clausum,*[15] the well-sealed vat — the discarded bottle cap implied in a mysterious way that our therapeutic relationship could no longer be an appropriate container for him. Without its Hermetic seal, the sanction of his unconscious, it could not function as a vessel for further transformation. This really was it, for his work with me. The patient would need a new analytic relationship.

The third, and final paradox: The dream depicts the actual situation in the unconscious, yet its symbolic language defends against direct insight into that situation and can be exploited by sophisticated defenses against taking its meaningful content seriously. The bottle cap, for instance, is such a banal image that it would probably not occur to any dreamer at first glance that this small synthetic circular object might be an image of the self, quite as important to individuation as any giant mandala. That it is synthetic suggests that the archetypal capacity to represent the Self had been forced into a restricting, artificial incarnation, in fact a false self for this particular dreamer. It took some work on our part to release the archetypal energies of the Self from this particular incarnation. Indeed, when the dreamer wrote "Try gestalt," and went through the exercise of associating in the gestalt way to the dream, he was confessing his perplexity and dissatisfaction with an apparently trivial image. It took my reading of these associations and a second and a third reading of them aloud by him to bring them into connection with the vital center of his own being. In other words, he was capable of a highly sophisticated symbolic dissociation, in a way fostered by the high-tech plastic dream symbol itself, which could have kept him from any genuine insight. Interpretation was needed, starting with a second and third reading of his associations—once more, with feeling—to get him out of an unrelated imaginal orbit and into a vital recognition that this was the image of his life.

When an interpretation really works—as it did with this man—it somehow manages to satisfy all three paradoxes. It lets the dreamer know his dream is alive, yet helps the dream bring an old attitude to its necessary death. It helps the dreamer find his own position within the therapeutic relationship, where perhaps analyst and patient have become unconsciously identified, yet respects the impersonal exigencies of the deep alchemical path of transformation with its unpredictable beginning, middle, and end of the analytic experiment. And finally the complete interpretation exposes the sophisticated defenses in order to permit access to the genuine existential immediacy of the dream.

In working with my patient's dream, I dealt with the defenses first, by arranging that between us we read his associations aloud three times. After that, we could both hear the dream, and I could disidentify with him enough to say, "But isn't that what you have been doing with your life?" implying that he might not need to confine himself any longer to such a rigidly heroic stance. The dreamer did the rest, by accepting the living reality of his dream and bringing his old, unsatisfactory way of living to an end.

Jungian analysis has been on the leading edge of this century's psychotherapy in understanding how affect and image can be brought together in the construction of integrity. When af-

fect and image are united, the archetype is released, a core of
energy that mysteriously participates in the integrative power
of the psyche that Jung called, after Indian philosophy, the Self.
It does not matter whether an affect comes first or an image.
In the case of my woman patient, exploration of her affect led
us to the conceptual image of her psychological type, a verbal
symbol that gave us a helpful way to think about her personality and set realistic goals for her life. In the case of my man
patient, exploration of a seemingly trivial dream image led to
a self-recognition that released his feeling for himself. In both
cases, the integrity of personality was constellated[16] by a careful attention to an emerging unconscious process.

A Fantasia on Integrity

The doctor who mediates this tremendous healing power today
has a tool that the philosopher and the minister and the novelist
have lacked in their efforts to improve integrity. That tool, delivered by way of Jung, is a conscious access to the archetype's
healing power. But what of the doctor who has found out how
to tap this healing power? What is the relation of the doctor's
personal integrity to the use of the unconscious to release a
blocked integrity? We have already touched on this question
in the first case, and perhaps my handling of my patient reflects
the fact that I have pondered this issue for a long time. I was
far less conscious of it when I first encountered material like
the dream I worked with in the second case, which may be
why my patient quickly outgrew his work with me.

When I first began to ponder the question of the doctor's
integrity in relation to the treatment, I came upon a fairy tale
in the Grimms' collection that speaks to this central issue, indeed to the point of being a fantasia on integrity. It is called
"The Three Army Surgeons":

The Three Army Surgeons

Three surgeons, who thought they had nothing more to learn about their art, were traveling from place to place. One night they stopped at an inn and the innkeeper asked them where they had come from and where they were going. "We are traveling surgeons," they said. "Show me what you can do," said the innkeeper. The first said he would cut off his hand and put it back on again in the morning, the second said he would tear out his heart and put it back again in the morning, and the third said he would cut out his eyes and put them back again in the morning. "If you can do that," said the innkeeper, "you have nothing more to learn." The fact is, they had an ointment which healed any wound they smeared with it and made the parts grow together, and wherever they went they carried this ointment with them. So they took a knife and the first surgeon cut off his hand, the second cut out his heart and the third his eyes just as they had said. Then they put them on a plate and gave them to the innkeeper, who told the servant girl to put them in the larder for safekeeping. Now the servant girl was secretly in love with a soldier, who came in when the innkeeper, the three surgeons, and everybody else in the house had gone to sleep, and asked for something to eat. The girl opened the larder and brought him something, but she was so be-fuddled with love that she forgot to close the door.

She sat down at the table with her sweetheart, and as they were sitting there, chatting away and suspecting no harm, the cat came creeping in, found the larder open, and made off with the hand, heart, and eyes of the three surgeons. When the soldier had finished eating and the girl thought she'd clear away the dishes and lock the larder, she saw that the plate the innkeeper had entrusted to her care was empty. She was frightened to death. "Lordy!" she cried. "What will I do now? The hand is gone, the heart and the eyes are gone too. What will they do to me tomorrow!" "Don't worry," said the soldier. "I know just what to do. There's a thief hanging on the gallows. I'll cut off his hand. Which hand was it?" "The right hand." The girl gave him a sharp knife and he went out, cut the hanged man's right hand off, and brought it in. Then he caught the cat and cut its eyes out. Only the heart was lacking. "Didn't you just butcher some pigs?" he asked. "Isn't the meat in the cellar?" "Yes," said the girl. "Then everything's fine and dandy," said the soldier, went down to the cellar and came back with a pig's heart. The girl laid all the things on a plate and put the plate in the larder. When her sweetheart had left her, she went calmly to bed.

When the surgeons got up in the morning, they asked the servant girl for the plate with the hand, heart, and eyes on it. She took it out of the larder and brought it to them. Whereupon the first put the thief's hand in place and rubbed it with the ointment, and instantly it grew onto his wrist. The second took the cat's eyes and fitted them into his eye sockets, and the third made the pig's heart fast. The innkeeper looked on and marveled at their skill. He said he'd never seen anything like it and promised to praise them and recommend them to everyone he met. Then they paid for their bed and board and started off.

Instead of walking with the others, the one with the pig's heart kept running into corners and rooting about like a pig. His comrades tried to hold him back by his coattails, but he persisted in breaking loose and running to the places where the garbage was deepest. The second was also behaving very oddly, rubbing his eyes and saying to the third: "Comrade, what's going on? These aren't my eyes, I can't see a thing. Lead me, one of you, or I'll fall." They dragged him painfully on until evening, and they came to another inn. They went to the public room together, and there in a corner sat a rich gentleman counting money. The surgeon with the thief's hand circled round him, and his hand kept twitching.

Finally, when the gentleman was looking the other way, the surgeon reached into the pile and took a handful of money. One of his friends saw him and said, "Hey, what are you doing? Stealing's not allowed. You ought to be ashamed!" "I can't help it," he said. "My hand twitches and in spite of myself I have to grab." Then they went to bed and it was so dark in their room that you couldn't see your hand before your face. Suddenly the one with the cat's eyes woke up, woke the other two, and said: "Hey brothers, look. Do you see those white mice running around?" The two of them sat up, but they couldn't see a thing. Then the one with the cat's eyes said: "There's something wrong with us. These aren't our organs. We'll have to go back to that innkeeper. He cheated us."

So next morning they started out and when they got there they told the innkeeper that they hadn't got their right organs back, that one had a thief's hand, the second a pig's heart, and the third cat's eyes. The innkeeper said only the servant girl could be to blame. He called her, but she wasn't there. She had seen the three surgeons coming and had run out the back door. The three said to the innkeeper: "Give us money and plenty of it, or we'll set fire to your house." He gave them as much as he could lay hands on, and they went their way. It was enough to last them the rest of their lives, but they'd sooner have had their proper organs.[17]

This is a tale that makes us laugh with rueful recognition even as we shudder at its gruesomeness. It reminds us of La Rochefoucauld's maxim that we are not entirely displeased to learn of the misfortunes of others, and there is something in it of Moliere, too. It is a comedy of the therapeutic impulse, in which the would-be doctors are the victims. Their fate makes us smile, and wince, because there is an overeager healer in all of us, easily manipulated by anyone who can talk us into a reckless display of the healing power we think we have at our disposal.

Since these are army surgeons, it is possible that what looks like a therapeutic impulse here is intended as a metaphor for military intervention. Remarkably similar considerations occur when a political entity's integrity is threatened and when personal integrity is at stake, a fact we have already met in the frequent use of political imagery in discussions of integrity. The various inns the surgeons stay at are like so many nations that welcome the idea of war; at such an inn the serving maid is indeed likely to fall in love with the soldier.

Military solutions are often presented as the lesser of two evils, the only way to achieve an eventual integrity even if the means seem drastic. But integrity can only be restored when there is containment, a condition that is rarely if ever met in war, which almost always spreads beyond its designated boundaries and inflicts unintended sacrifices. Whatever the ultimate referent, the dire consequences of failed containment are reinforced by the tale of the three army surgeons, and the surgeons do at the end seem like wounded veterans of combat.

The centrality of containment for the achievement of integrity is the point of Jung's emphasis in his studies of alchemy on the well-sealed vessel. In the laboratory of psychotherapy, our century has rediscovered this symbol as central for the healing of integrity. In therapy, as we have seen, the sealed container is the emblem of the therapeutic relationship, which is built up with great care over time as the participants get to know and trust each other. Working on integrity in such a relationship demands that the doctor eventually relinquish control, like these three surgeons who voluntarily remove their hand, heart, and eyes. Asked how he did psychotherapy, the late Ronald Laing said, "I don't know, I make myself vulnerable and see what happens."[18]

We would be wrong to read our story as a criticism of the surgeons for daring to relinquish so much of themselves in the service of healing. All therapists have to do the same. What we should fault them for is attending so little to the containing environment of the work. Our surgeons are so naive in their approach to this problem, one feels like leaping into the story to give them supervision.

Making oneself as vulnerable as I did to my long-term woman patient is possible, or desirable, only in a mutually containing relationship. I could defer to my second patient's dream only because I had worked at every conscious level to understand the totality of his life situation and in the process had become deeply immersed in his dilemma, which contained both of us. Then I was willing to let his dream, as the voice of his own deepest conscience, tell him, and me, what he should do.

By contrast, our surgeons simply come to an inn and are led into a display of their ability to restore integrity. They have little relationship with the innkeeper, still less with the serving maid who is supposed to keep their organs in the larder overnight, and none at all with the cat who makes off with their sacrificed sensibilities. No wonder things turn out badly! I have not included in these accounts my own examples of therapeutic failure, when my narcissism led me to believe I "had nothing more to learn about my art," but they involved a similar lack of attention to the honest building of a containing relationship before the risky work on integrity was attempted.

We can compare the honoring of the ideal relationship in the psychotherapeutic transference to the opus that emerges from other forms of devotion to the ideal, like Cicero's love of Greek philosophy, Milton's submission to God, and Jane Austen's feeling for the men the English Navy selected for its officers. In each case something very like a transference is served not passively, but actively; through Cicero's own philosophy, Milton's poetry, Jane Austen's novels, a conscious relationship to the idealized object gradually replaces the idealizing impulse and integrity emerges. An idealizing transference is served by taking it seriously enough to get to know the object of it well, and a relationship that is built up by following the unconscious in this way has itself great integrity. Once achieved, the relationship can be the holding environment for the discovery of an even more radical integrity, which feels like the grace of God. In the tale, this radical integrity is mediated by the healing ointment. But a stage has been skipped, and the ointment does not truly serve the partners in the enterprise.

It is clear that the relationship the surgeons primarily lack is to themselves. There are no patients in the story, and the inn is like a temporary office where the surgeons set up shop. Beyond the danger of taking the need for a containing environment so lightly is the fact that so many aspects of it function out of the surgeons' awareness. If we make the tale an allegory of therapy, the maid, the soldier, and the cat might be parts of the therapist which are out of control in the countertransference.

Psychotherapy has been a laboratory for our culture to learn more about working on integrity, and findings from this setting have started to enter the broader traditions of literature, religion, and moral philosophy. Before we give the baby of integrity back to its rightful parents, however, depth psychology needs to relay all that it has learned about integrity's care. I have already put the central discovery in the language of Chinese philosophy: *te* is as important as Tao.

In our tale, however, Tao triumphs over *te,* which is why it's a black comedy. No one makes an attempt to act with integrity; the surgeons' body parts that are compromised are organs of *te.* (In the Ma-wang-tui manuscripts of the *Tao Te Ching,* the graph for *te* was composed of an eye and a heart.) The ointment is the Tao. It works "without purpose/Yet nothing remains unfurthered."

For this Western tale, the Stoic spirit of universal order is an even nearer gloss. The ointment is like the *pneuma* imagined by the Stoics as the breath of God pervading the universe, "a binding force" and "an agent which generates all the physical qualities of matter."[19] According to the Stoic conception, the "basic function of the pneuma is the generation of the cohesion of matter and generally of the contact between all parts of the cosmos."[20] The *pneuma* was also in the body. The ointment is something the surgeons can simply smear on body parts to make them knit together, and it is a sort of concentrated *pneuma,* an archetypal capacity to promote integrity.[21]

The capacity to promote integrity gets concentrated in particular disciplines at different times. It was the prerogative of the philosopher in Cicero's day, of the poet in Milton's, of the statesman in Franklin's time, and of the novelist in the nineteenth century. Since Freud and Jung, this concentration of healing power has been in the hands of the depth psychologist.

Like the three surgeons, the great cultural healers engage our attention by showing us what has been entrusted in their discipline and letting us see their willingness to submit to it. Jung's obvious sincerity makes his discussion of *wu wei* glow in his 1929 "Commentary on The Secret of the Golden Flower."[22] There he first formulated the idea of the Self, and this was the book which brought Jungian analysts into the central habit of trusting the Tao. Jung's advice that "consciousness is forever interfering, helping, correcting, and negating, never leaving the psychic processes to grow in peace" has made a dent in our culture's sense of how integrity can be worked on.

But there is more to following the unconscious with integrity than letting things happen. When therapists, like the three surgeons, trust the Tao so much that they assume that it will bring order by itself, they are repaid with a compromised order: the maid leaves the larder door open because she is too love-struck with the soldier to remember to close it, and the cat creeps in and makes off with the organs of discrimination. For love of a soldier, the humane faculties depart, and a compromise of integrity occurs. Again we are led to consider the danger of military shortcuts to integrity. In war the normal human sensibilities of hand, heart, and eye are temporarily suspended in the service of the higher goal of eventually restoring a better integrity. But when do they come back?

The tale suggests that the surgeons' risk would be justified had the anima associated with the inn been truly mature.[23] Integrity might still be possible in a war conducted with Confucian sincerity and followed, on Lao Tzu's advice, by a funeral at its end instead of a victory celebration. The best image we have in the West of sustained integrity in war is Abraham Lincoln. When the anima is not mature, a nation's emotional tendency, like the maid's in this tale, is to fall in love with the soldier and to fail to guard the organs of *te*. Then integrity is compromised, consciousness is devoured, and military ruthlessness has its say in shaping the new attitudes that appear. Compromises are enemies of integrity, even though at first they seem quite naturally to lock into place. In the tale these compromises of integrity are symbolized by the thief's hand, the pig's heart, and the cat's eyes — what a therapist would describe as primitive greed, a morbid interest in the shadow, and paranoia. These are frequent moods of postwar disillusionment, but they follow any effort at integrity that has been poorly contained. I have experienced such moods as the countertransference residue of work with patients that did not go well, and I accept them as consequences of my failures in taking proper care of the therapeutic environment.

To make work on integrity succeed, a cultivated *te* is necessary, and this cannot take place without relationship — which means relationship to others, to self, to culture. Relationship to the humane was the meaning, for Cicero, of *humanitas*. When this relationship fails in therapy, only a hard, penetrating look at the resistance will help.

Yet failures in relationship also serve integrity, and we cannot simply read "The Three Army Surgeons" as a cautionary story about what happens when *te* is not contained and the Tao is forced to support a compromise of integrity. There is also cunning in the story, for it demonstrates the tragic nature of any work on integrity. Here, *Hamlet* rather than Cicero is the more reliable guide. We see why Shakespeare jibes at Cicero in his portrait of Polonius. Real work on integrity means more than taking the lofty position, it also includes accepting the shadow and taking the impure parts of the collective human and animal character consciously into oneself.

Our army surgeons are forced to recognize parts of the thief, the pig, and the cat in themselves, and this difficult confrontation leads to a more conscious relationship to envy, shame, and anxiety. They also experience rage at the innkeeper's failure to stand for the ideal of containment, and rage, as we have seen, is a step to the healthy self that can defend its integrity.

Nevertheless, the would-be healers of integrity are left with a longing for wholeness. But even that is an improvement. Gone is the inflated reliance upon the power of Tao eventually to set things right. Instead, the chastened recognition of compromised integrity has produced a hunger for genuine healing. I would wish these wounded healers an active patience.

Epilogue

ST. THOMAS AQUINAS appreciated the power and the beauty of the Latin word *integritas*. Perhaps it implied for him not only the possibility of wholeness but also the active sense in us which knows when we are deviating from that possibility. On another topic he wrote, "We do not know what God is, but only what He is not, and what relation everything else has with Him."[1] A developed sensitivity to the needs of the whole is what I have meant by integrity, which I see as brought by psychological consciousness to a preexisting archetype of completeness.

To use what is becoming an old-fashioned simile, I have often envisioned the wholeness of a life as a long-playing record, and integrity as the diamond stylus that tracks the grooves of the record. The diamond body on which the release of the music depends is not a simple achievement. It has been created by intense pressure on carbon atoms and cut and shaped by human effort. Yet it is the diamond itself, the sensitive capacity to embrace the whole and accord fidelity to all its parts, that actually gives the musical pleasure. In these pages I have tried to depict the psychological forces that produce the diamond of integrity and to convey how the practice of psychotherapy affords the opportunity to enjoy integrity's fidelity to the whole.

Recently, a patient described a dream in which he was an orchestra conductor, walking down a hallway backstage where there were a lot of practice rooms of musicians. He was explaining to someone the orchestra's structure of rehearsing, under which musicians worked individually by themselves. Through the walls of the practice rooms, one could hear that some of the musicians were very good, some not so good. Even though that was the case, when they came together with their varying degrees of musicianship as an ensemble, they made extraordinarily beautiful music, fuller and more pleasing than any of them could produce separately. To be present for an honest engagement of the entirety of personality is always intensely satisfying, and psychotherapy offers a setting where the mystery of that entirety can be appreciated.

In his monumental study of the human life cycle, Erik Erikson concluded that ego integrity was the highest achievement of the final stage of maturity, and that it offered an alternative to despair. In a lecture given in San Francisco in 1960 he said:

> Ego strength in the old means the ability to maintain the wholeness of the personality even as the body gradually falls apart and again becomes a conglomerate of parts which now weaken, as they once matured, at different rates. Only a certain integrity can save the old from a gnawing despair. But if a certain vigor of mind combines with the gift of responsible renunciation, some old people can envisage human problems in their entirety, which is what integrity means, and express the principles involved.[2]

My work with patients spans the thirty years since Erikson made these remarks, and it has been with people from a highly psychological generation. It has seemed that although the ability to see things in their entirety develops only slowly, the will to make the effort appears much earlier. Clinical experience has led me to a conviction: each time a willing receptivity to the whole emerges, I know that integrity has surfaced out of its prior life in depth.

Notes

CHAPTER 1. A PSYCHOLOGICAL DEFINITION OF INTEGRITY

1. David Michael Levin, *The Body's Recollection of Being* (London: Routledge & Kegan Paul, 1985), pp. 270–71.

2. Michael Grant, Introduction, in Cicero, *On the Good Life* (London: Penguin Books, 1971), p. 21.

3. Cicero, "Against Verres: Part Two" in *The Verrine Orations*, trans. L. H. G. Greenwood (Cambridge: Harvard University Press, Loeb Classical Library, 1928), Volume 1, Book One, II, para. 4–5.

4. They were never delivered. "Verres exercised a Roman's privilege of retiring into exile in the middle of the trial. Cicero clinched his victory by publishing the series of speeches which, in theory at least, he would have delivered if Verres had stayed the course." D. R. Shackleton Bailey, *Cicero* (New York: Charles Scribner's, 1971), pp. 16–17.

5. Gary Lindberg, *The Confidence Man in American Literature* (New York: Oxford University Press, 1982), p. 83.

6. Benjamin Franklin, *The Autobiography* (New York: Library of America, 1987), pp. 1384–85, 1386–87, 1392.

7. Ibid., p. 1393.

8. Donald Earl, *The Moral and Political Tradition of Rome* (Ithaca, N.Y.: Cornell University Press, 1967), pp. 44–58. The basic attitudes of Cicero's society are well summarized in Harry G. Edinger's introduction to his translation of Cicero's *De Officiis* (Indianapolis: Bobbs-Merrill, 1974), pp. ix–xxix.

128

9. As Neal Wood puts it, "Caesar's death gave Cicero one last political opportunity, and during the first half of 43 [B.C.], if anyone can claim the distinction, he was the virtual ruler of Rome in the name of liberation from tyranny. But his ferocious — and, as it proved, highly imprudent — onslaught against Marc Antony in the thirteen *Philippics,* named after Demosthenes' passionate attack against Philip of Macedonia three centuries before, sealed his fate. . . . Cicero and his allies were proscribed by the new junta, and after several vacillating and vain efforts to flee Italy he was murdered by their soldiers on December 7, 43." Neal Wood, *Cicero's Social and Political Thought* (Berkeley: University of California Press, 1988), p. 54.

10. Robert Grudin, *Time and the Art of Living* (New York: Ticknor & Fields, 1988), p. 51.

11. Cicero, unlike Franklin, had been on the wrong side politically. When Julius Caesar came to power after the defeat and assassination of the Republic's last consul, Pompey, Cicero retired to write about the values he had not been successful in getting Rome to live by. Among the numerous philosophical works he produced between 46 and 44 B.C., the one which has found widest favor across the centuries (until our own) has been *De Officiis.* This book is the most practical manual for success through integrity ever written. Perhaps Cicero was experiencing a final burst of hope, since the book was begun in the summer of 44 B.C., a few months after the assassination of Caesar on the fifteenth of March, when Brutus, drawing out his sword, had cried "Cicero!" Cicero might have imagined that his own reputation for integrity would be enough to enable him to restore the Republic. During the last half of that fateful year, he waited for a call back to public life, occupying himself by writing *De Officiis.*

12. Michael Grant, headnote to selection from *De Officiis* in Cicero, *On the Good Life,* p. 117.

13. Wood, *Cicero's Social and Political Thought,* p. 68.

14. Cicero, *De Officiis,* II, xii, 43, trans. Grant in *On The Good Life,* pp. 141–42.

15. Peter Green, *Alexander to Actium: The Historical Evolution of the Hellenistic Age* (Berkeley: University Of California Press, 1990),

chap. 36, "Stoicism: The Wide and Sheltering Porch," pp. 631–46. Green's position is that Stoicism, the Hellenistic synthesis of all earlier philosophic thought, was not only compatible with the Roman character, it was to become the rationalization for the selfishness of its oligarchy in the early Empire.

16. Cicero, *De Officiis,* III, iii, 13, trans. Michael Grant in *Selected Works* (London: Penguin Books, 1971), p. 163, emphasis in the original. This arose (Grant informs us) with "Chrysippus, the third head of the Stoic school, [who] had added 'with nature' to Zeno's original formula 'to live consistently.'"

17. Cicero, *De Officiis,* I, xxx, 107, trans. Harry Edinger (Indianapolis: Bobbs-Merrill, 1974), pp. 49–50.

18. Cicero, *De Officiis,* I, xxxi, 110, as rendered by Emile Brehier, translated from the French by Wade Baskin, in *The Hellenistic and Roman Age* (Chicago: University of Chicago Press, 1965), p. 132. Edinger (p. 52) translates this passage somewhat differently, as follows: "We have the obligation to act in such a way that we do not put ourselves in opposition to nature in general, and yet we must follow our particular nature without violating the general one. Even if other pursuits are more important and attractive, we should nevertheless measure our own ambitions against the yardstick of our own nature."

Walter Miller (Cambridge: Harvard University Press, Loeb Classical Library, 1913), p. 113, translates it as: "For we must so act as not to oppose the universal laws of human nature, but, while safeguarding those, to follow the bent of our own particular nature; and even if other careers should be better and nobler, we may still regulate our own pursuits by the standard of our own nature."

According to Brehier, what Cicero meant by living in accord with nature was what Clement of Alexandria, two hundred years later, described as "to live according to the inclinations that nature has given us."

19. Brehier is of this opinion (*Hellenistic and Roman Age,* p. 132). Panaetius's treatise was written in 140 B.C. Peter Green, in his discussion of stoicism in *Alexander to Actium,* points to the way such a phi-

losophy was "tailor made" to serve the aspirations of the commercial aristocrats of the late Republic and early Empire: "Act in consonance with human nature as a whole, and your own nature in particular: the *De Officiis* may not have been written as a handbook for self-deceivers (any more than Panaetius's lost work *On Duty*, which formed its source), but on occasion it reads remarkably like it" (pp. 641–42).

Cicero, like many another writer about to make a new discovery, may have believed he was merely completing the thought of his teacher. Panaetius, who had left his own analysis of moral obligations incomplete, initially had thought to pose three questions as a way to discriminate moral obligations. (We have to take Cicero's word for this, because Panaetius's *On Duties*, which he claimed was his model, no longer exists.) "1. Is a thing morally right or wrong? 2. Is it advantageous or disadvantageous? 3. If apparent right and apparent advantage clash, what is to be the basis for our choice between them?" Cicero, *De Officiis*, III, ii, 7, trans. Grant in *Selected Works*, p. 161.

Complaining to his son, as everyone who has ever looked for guidance as to the nature of integrity has complained, that the big question, number 3, remained unanswered, Cicero tells us: "Panaetius wrote a three-part treatise about the first two of these questions; the third question he said he would deal with in its proper turn. But he never fulfilled his promise. This seems to me all the more surprising because he was still alive thirty years after the publication of the first three parts of his work—his pupil Posidonius records this. Posidonius himself briefly refers to the subject in certain notes, but it seems to me strange that he, too, did not deal with it at greater length. For he expressed the opinion that there is no more vital theme in the whole range of philosophy." *De Officiis*, III, ii, 7–8, pp. 161–62.

For Cicero the basis of our choice between an apparent right and apparent advantage to ourselves is our integrity. Because this is the basis of all the rest of our morality, we have to cultivate and learn to defend that part of ourselves, as well as to promote its recognition in the world.

20. Seneca, *Letters*, 120: 3–5, 8–11, in A. A. Long & D. N. Sedley, *The Hellenistic Philosophers. Volume 1: Translations of the Principal Sources*

with Philosophical Commentary (Cambridge: Cambridge University Press, 1987), pp. 369–70. I am grateful to Professor Long himself for pointing out this reference to me.

21. Cicero, *De Officiis*, III, xxxiii, 118, trans. Edinger, p. 178.

22. One of the best discussions of Aquinas's conception of *integritas* is by Umberto Eco in his *The Aesthetics of Thomas Aquinas*, trans. Hugh Bredin (Cambridge: Harvard University Press, 1988), pp. 98–102.

In the last chapter of James Joyce's *A Portrait of the Artist as a Young Man*, Stephen Dedalus expands in an exuberant, scholastic way, on Aquinas's idea of *integritas*, making it mean the perceived nature of a thing as "selfbounded and selfcontained upon the immeasurable background of space or time which is not it." (New York: Penguin Books, 1964), p. 212. For an elaboration of this passage in Joyce, see Joseph Campbell, "Creativity," in *C. G. Jung and the Humanities*, ed. Karin Barnaby and Pellegrino D'Acierno (Princeton, N.J.: Princeton University Press, 1990), p. 142.

23. Mark S. Halfon, *Integrity: A Philosophical Inquiry* (Philadelphia: Temple University Press, 1989), p. 4. John Rawls is unusually generous in his discussion of integrity when he stops in the midst of a several-hundred-page treatise on the nature of justice to give integrity a short paragraph. There he at least gives a reason for the neglect by moral philosophers: "In times of social doubt and loss of faith in long established values, there is a tendency to fall back on the virtues of integrity: truthfulness and sincerity, lucidity and commitment, or as some say, authenticity. . . . Now of course the virtues of integrity are virtues, and among the excellences of free persons. Yet while necessary, they are not sufficient. . . . It is impossible to construct a moral view from these virtues alone; being virtues of form they are in a sense secondary. But joined to the appropriate conception of justice, one that allows for autonomy and objectivity correctly understood, they come into their own." John Rawls, *A Theory of Justice* (Cambridge: Harvard University Press, Belknap Press, 1971), pp. 519–20.

24. Quote by Andrew Oldenquist, Ohio State University, from jacket of Halfon, *Integrity*.

25. For instance, Gabriele Taylor, "Integrity," in her *Pride, Shame and Guilt: Emotions of Self-Assessment* (Oxford: Clarendon Press, 1985), pp. 108–41; Lynne McFall, "Integrity," *Ethics* 98/1 (Oct., 1987): 5–20; Martin Benjamin, *Splitting the Difference: Compromise and Integrity in Ethics and Politics* (Lawrence: University Press of Kansas, 1990); Michael S. Pritchard, *On Becoming Responsible* (Lawrence: University Press of Kansas, 1991); and Owen Flanagan, "Abstraction, Alienation and Integrity," in his *Varieties of Moral Personality* (Cambridge: Harvard University Press, 1991), pp. 79–101.

26. Robert Grudin, *The Grace of Great Things* (New York: Ticknor & Fields, 1990), pp. 73–75.

27. The person in the classical world who most typifies what Cicero was seeking to impart is Socrates, whose charm (and strangeness) derive from the pleasure he takes in his integrity. See Gregory Vlastos, *Socrates: Ironist and Moral Philosopher* (Ithaca, N.Y.: Cornell University Press, 1991), esp. pp. 233–35.

28. William Willeford, *Feeling, Imagination, and the Self* (Evanston, Ill.: Northwestern University Press, 1987), pp. 31–32.

29. Michael Fordham, *The Objective Psyche* (London: Routledge and Kegan Paul, 1958), chapter entitled "The Dark Night of the Soul," pp. 130–48.

30. *Intersubjectivity* is a recent word from self-psychology that defines the shared field of integrity in which one person extends the selfhood of another. The assumption that the self becomes itself only in relation to others can be traced back to John Dewey's emphasis on experience and George Herbert Mead's postulate that the self consists of reflected appraisals. Harry Stack Sullivan developed this therapeutically in his idea of participant observation. Then came Carl Rogers's careful research into clients' responses to their therapists' reflections of their feelings, which demonstrated that in addition to offering empathy a therapist needed to be someone the patient saw as genuine and as a provider of unconditional positive regard. Across the Atlantic, D. W. Winnicott's work on the holding environment revealed that the patient holds the analyst as much as the analyst holds the patient. Continuing another line of thought beginning with Al-

fred Adler and Otto Rank, Abraham Maslow presented self-actual-
ization as the consequence and the impetus of an optimally supportive personal environment. Heinz Kohut's recent conception of the
self as an intersubjective phenomenon requiring the selfobject's capacity for empathy and introspection to find and facilitate its unfolding is but the latest in this series of discoveries about the interpersonal
nature of our integrity.

During the entire course of this development, Jung, little noticed
by American psychiatry, developed his own interactional, empathic,
introspective, and intersubjective way of holding patients within an
analytic container in which a sense of personal integration might make
its appearance. He carefully recorded the symbolism of what he found,
noticing an emphasis on boundedness, containment, privacy, all of
which indicated a central concern with integrity. Jung's work gave
boundaries and definitions to what else was happening in European
psychotherapy at the same time, the work of the existentialists, with
their notion of authentic encounter and facilitation of the "I am" experience. The existentialists emphasized the personally felt meaning,
rather than the symbolism, of integrity, and so their viewpoint translated more easily into the consciousness of American psychotherapists than Jung's. One cannot appreciate any of these theorists, however, without noticing the profound pleasure all of them take in the
integrity of the self which has been revealed to them in these various ways.

31. Heinz Kohut, "Thoughts on Narcissism and Narcissistic Rage,"
in Paul Ornstein, ed., *The Search for the Self* (New York: International Universities Press, 1978), II, 615–58; Robert Langs, *The Listening Process* (New York: Jason Aronson, 1978); Jeffrey Moussaieff Masson, *The Assault on Truth* (New York: Viking Press, Penguin Books,
1985).

32. William B. Goodheart, "Theory of Analytic Interaction," *San
Francisco Jung Institute Library Journal* 1/4 (Summer, 1980): 2–39. The
article stresses the therapist's integrity as well as the patient's. It is
Goodheart's view "that in a complex-discharging field the unconscious
and undifferentiated archetypal cores of the complexes are channelled

134

through the complex-discharging efforts and 'overload' the analytic relationship with unconscious archetypal demands or expectations or lack of expectations. The analyst or the patient then 'ask' that archetypal qualities be present in the other which are present only in the mythopoeic Gods and Goddesses. Archetypal demands do not recognize human boundaries, as Jung strongly emphasized, but rather expand or depreciate them. They blot out the fundamental awareness of the integrity of the other, either from the side of his strengths or from the side of his limits. One of the most sensitive monitors we have that this 'overload' has occurred is when we begin to feel a lack of integrity within ourselves or view or treat the patient as being without integrity or feel moved to violate the integrity of the container" (p. 21).

33. John Bradshaw, *Healing the Shame That Binds You* (Deerfield Beach, Fla.: Health Communications, 1988); John Bradshaw, *Homecoming* (New York: Bantam, 1990).

34. C. G. Jung, *Psychological Types,* Vol. 6 of *Collected Works* (Princeton, N.J.: Princeton University Press, 1971). The German original, *Psychologische Typen* (Zurich: Rascher Verlag, 1921), was translated into English by H. G. Baynes with Jung's approval carrying the subtitle "The Psychology of Individuation" (London: Kegan Paul; New York: Harcourt Brace, 1923).

35. This is the title of the second chapter of Willeford, *Feeling, Imagination, and Self,* p. 27.

36. When feeling is the superior function of an individual, the compass of psychological types would look like the accompanying figure.

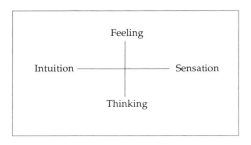

The vertical line, whose endpoints are feeling and thinking, is the rational axis; the horizontal line between intuition and sensation defines this person's irrational axis. If, on the other hand, a person has an irrational function such as sensation as the superior function, then the vertical line would be the irrational (sensation-intuition) axis and the rational (feeling-thinking) axis would be the horizontal. The implications for psychological orientation of having a rational or an irrational function as the superior function are profound.

37. "Le coeur a ses raisons que la raison ne connait point. . . ." Blaise Pascal, *Pensees,* Vol. 13 in *Oeuvres de Blaise Pascal,* ed. Leon Brunschvicg (Paris: Librairie Hachette, 1904) IV, 277, p. 201. English translation, *The Concise Oxford Dictionary of Quotations* (New York: Oxford University Press, 1981), p. 181. Pascal's use of *heart* seems to identify feeling with irrational intuition. Elsewhere in the *Pensees* he says "Those who are accustomed to judge by feeling do not understand the process of reasoning, for they would understand at first sight, and are not used to seek for principles." *Pensees,* trans. W. F. Trotter (New York: Random House, 1941) I, 3, p. 5. I am indebted to Joseph Wheelwright for recognizing the importance of Jung's break with this tradition.

38. See I. N. Marshall, "The Four Functions: A Conceptual Analysis," *Journal of Analytical Psychology* 13/1 (1968): 1–32.

39. James Yandell, personal communication.

40. Joseph Henderson, "The Psychic Activity of Dreaming," *Psychological Perspectives* 3/2 (1972): 104–105.

41. According to this theory, psyche makes itself known through images and affects that partake of a common source in the "collective" unconscious, the archetypes, which carry the potential for forming human instinctual energies into commonly recognizable patterns that can either become programs of behavior or conscious realizations, or both. Jung asserts that all archetypes are part of, and under the control of, the central organizing archetype, which also represents their totality of intention, the Self.

42. Jung, *Psychological Types,* p. 214, para. 358.

43. C. G. Jung, "The Relations between the Ego and the Uncon-

scious," in *Two Essays on Analytical Psychology,* Vol. 7, 2nd ed., rev., of *Collected Works* (Princeton, N.J.: Princeton University Press, 1966), p. 154, para. 241.

44. Lao Tzu, *Tao Teh King,* trans. Archie J. Bahm (New York: Frederick Ungar Publishing Company, 1958), p. 26.

45. Victor H. Mair, "Preface" to his translation of Lao Tzu, *Tao Te Ching: The Classic Book of Integrity and the Way* (New York: Bantam, 1990), pp. xii–xiv. This new rendering is based on the Mawang-tui manuscripts discovered in 1973. Professor Mair (personal communication) has pointed out that this conception of *te* as integrity is accurate only for the early Taoist period of these manuscripts, which date from approximately 200 B.C. In the Confucian period, the traditional translation of *te* as virtue is more appropriate.

46. Ibid., pp. 134–35.

47. Ibid.

48. Hellmut Wilhelm, *Heaven, Earth, and Man in the Book of Changes* (Seattle: University of Washington Press, 1977), p. 13. Ian McMorran, an expert on Wang Fu-chih (Wang Fuzhi), has told me that the term translated here as integrity is *ch'eng* which is often translated as sincerity. A. C. Graham, however, in his discussion of the philosophy of Ch'eng Yi-ch'uan, points out that the meaning is "accomplish, complete" and that "it seems preferable to translate it by 'integrity.'" He explains that in Sung (Song) philosophy "To be *ch'eng* is to be an integral whole, all of one piece. According to the *Doctrine of the Mean,* 'Integrity is self-completion' on which Yi-ch'uan comments: '. . . Thus if you serve your parents with complete integrity, you are a complete son; if your ruler, you are a complete minister.'" A. C. Graham, *Two Chinese Philosophers* (London: Humphries, 1958), p. 67. I am indebted to Professor McMorran (personal communication) for this reference. He explains that Wang Fu-chih's "openness to connections" is "something of a combination of" classically neo-Confucian terms Graham translates as integrity (*ch'eng*) and composure (*ching*). These concepts are found in the eleventh-century philosophy of Ch'eng Yi-ch'uan and the twelfth-century synthesis of neo-Confucian ideas by Chu Hsi (Zhu Xi).

49. That it is possible to focus on this "felt sense" is the basis of integrity's entry into psychological consciousness. For the interface between philosophy and psychology that "felt meaning" represents, see Eugene Gendlin, *Experiencing and the Creation of Meaning* (New York: Free Press, 1962), and Gendlin's description of a technique for allowing the felt sense to unfold, *Focusing* (New York: Bantam, 1981).

CHAPTER 2. THE SHADOW AND INTEGRITY

1. Sean Hand, "Preface" to Emmanuel Levinas, *The Levinas Reader* (Cambridge, Mass.: Basil Blackwell, 1989), p. v.

2. Erich Neumann was the first Jungian analyst to point out the need to examine the ethical consequences of depth psychology's discovery of the shadow. Erich Neumann, *Depth Psychology and a New Ethic* (Boston: Shambhala, 1990).

3. Emmanuel Levinas, "Ethics as First Philosophy" in *Levinas Reader,* p. 86.

4. The interested reader can pursue a lively discussion of these terms in Edward Edinger's *Ego and Archetype* (Baltimore: Penguin Books, 1973). There (p. 3), he defines the ego as "the center of the conscious personality" and the Self as "the ordering and unifying center of the total psyche (conscious and unconscious)." He says, "The ego is the seat of *subjective* identity while the Self is the seat of *objective* identity." He describes an "ego-Self axis" as the "vital connecting link between ego and Self that ensures the integrity of the ego" (p. 6). It is along this axis that I locate the deeper integrity that I am discussing throughout this book. Personal shadow, archetypal shadow, and absolute evil are different layers of threat to that integrity from unrecognized unconscious forces.

5. Marie-Louise von Franz, *Individuation in Fairy Tales* (Boston: Shambhala Publications, 1990), p. 206.

6. C. G. Jung, "To Arnold Kunzli" in *Letters,* ed. Gerhard Adler and Aniela Jaffe, trans. R. F. C. Hull (Princeton, N.J.: Princeton University Press, 1973), p. 333.

7. Jerome D. Frank, *Persuasion and Healing* (New York: Schocken, 1963).

8. Translation by Gary Massey, in Liliane Frey-Rohn, *Friedrich Nietzsche: A Psychological Approach to His Life and Work* (Einsiedeln, Switzerland: Daimon Verlag, 1988), p. 47. The original German quote is from volume 2, part 2 (*The Wanderer and His Shadow*) of Friedrich Nietzsche, *Werke: Kritische Gesamtausgabe,* ed. Giorgio Colli and Mazzino Montinari (Berlin: De Gruyter, 1967–), pp. 542–43, aphorism 6.

9. Ibid., p. 47. The original German is from Friedrich Nietzsche, *Werke: Kritische Gesamtausgabe,* vol. 8, *Nachgelassen Werke 1875–1879,* p. 588. Nearly the same sentiment is expressed in aphorism 16 of *The Wanderer and His Shadow.* At the end of the book, The Shadow confides to the philosophizing Wanderer, "Of all you have said nothing has pleased me *more* than a promise you have made: you want again to become a good neighbour to the things closest to you. This will benefit us poor shadows, too. For—admit it— you have hitherto been only too happy to slander us." Friedrich Nietzsche, "The Wanderer and His Shadow," in *Human, All Too Human,* trans. R. J. Hollingdale (New York: Cambridge University Press, 1986), p. 394.

10. In a more religious age it was apparent that an attitude of integrity was a gift from God. King David, following his sin of sending Uriah, the husband of Bathsheba, to his death in battle so that he might have his own marriage with this loyal general's wife, prayed (Psalm 51) for forgiveness by asking that his integrity be improved: "Behold, thou desirest truth in the inward parts; and in the hidden part thou shalt make me know wisdom." But Nietzsche does not presuppose a God who will intervene; with an arrogant optimism the youthful philosopher assumes that human beings will *want* to accept truth where they have been self-deceived. This is not the religious, or even the psychological view of the matter, which the mature Nietzsche would adopt with mounting pessimism.

11. In section 36 of *The Antichrist* (1888), he writes, "Only we, we spirits who have *become free,* have the presuppositions for understanding something that nineteen centuries have misunderstood: that

integrity which, having become instinct and passion, wages war against the 'holy lie' even more than against any other lie." Trans. Walter Kaufmann, in *The Portable Nietzsche* (New York: Viking Press, 1954), p. 609.

12. *The I Ching or Book of Changes.* The Richard Wilhelm Translation Rendered into English by Cary F. Baynes. 3rd ed. (Princeton, N.J.: Princeton University Press, 1977), p. 55.

13. C. G. Jung, *The Practice of Psychotherapy,* Vol. 16, 2nd ed., rev., of *Collected Works* (Princeton, N.J.: Princeton University Press, 1966), p. 87, para. 196.

14. Leo Rangell, *The Mind of Watergate: An Exploration of the Compromise of Integrity* (New York: W. W. Norton, 1980).

15. Robert Cummings Neville, *The Puritan Smile: A Look toward Moral Reflection* (Albany: State University of New York Press, 1987), p. 115. Professor Neville lists four dimensions of moral discernment. The first is the imagination for forming options. The second is the formation of choices by constructing "a ranking of the options with an articulation of the reasons that would justify the choice." The third is "the process of developing an inclusive vision that treats the various rankings as perspectives and finds some way of relating them." The fourth "is a combination of what Plato called dialectic and the Confucians called sincerity. On the one hand it is the process of moving back and forth to identify, articulate, and assess each of the previously mentioned steps in moral discernment, noting especially what values are distorted or dropped out in the process of discernment. . . . On the other hand, the judgments involved in this back and forth movement, while criticizable after the fact, arise out of an antecedent formation of character. The judgments need to be sensitive, perspicacious, faithful in remembering what has gone before, and directed with an open hope for finding the best reason rather than a rationalization for secret motives." Ibid., pp. 113–15.

16. Charles Brenner, *An Elementary Textbook of Psycho-analysis* (New York: Doubleday Anchor, 1955), p. 128.

17. Neville, *Puritan Smile,* pp. 1, 4.

18. T. S. Eliot, *On Poetry and Poets* (New York: Farrar, Straus and

Cudahy, 1957), p. 168. Eliot's idea (p. 139) that a "dissociation of sensibility" between thought and feeling occurred at this time is less interesting to me than his intuition of post-traumatic stress as a consequence of the brief Puritan ascendancy. A full discussion of this controversial subject can be found in Patrick Murray, *Milton: The Modern Phase; A Study of Twentieth-century Criticism* (New York: Barnes and Noble, 1967), Chapter 3, "Dissociation of Sensibility," pp. 31-49.

19. Tony Davies, Introduction to his edition of *John Milton: Selected Shorter Poems and Prose Writings* (London: Routledge, 1988), pp. 13, 19.

20. Douglas Bush, Introduction to his edition of *The Portable Milton* (New York: Viking Penguin, 1977), p. 1.

21. Tony Davies, "Critical Commentary," in *John Milton: Selected Shorter Poems and Prose Writings,* p. 175.

22. Milton, "How soon hath Time, the subtle thief of youth," in Davies, *John Milton: Selected Shorter Poems and Prose Writings,* p. 124.

23. Marina Warner, personal communication. She considers integrity, like virginity, the *sine qua non* of a virtue's being a virtue in the first place. See pp. 77-78 and my discussion of "the sieve of Tuccia," pp. 50-53.

24. Adolf Guggenbühl-Craig, "Puritanism," in *Psychic Reality and the Spirit of Jung in the 1990s* (Los Angeles: Proceedings of the National Conference of Jungian Analysts, October, 1990), p. 55.

25. Christopher Hill, *Milton and the English Revolution* (New York: Viking Press, 1977), p. 124. In the midst of the severe criticism these pamphlets endured, Milton wrote his *Areopagitica,* which retains its reputation as the greatest defense of the freedom of the press to be found in the English language.

26. John Milton, *Doctrine and Discipline of Divorce* (London, 1643), quoted in Hill, *Milton and the English Revolution* (New York: Viking Press, 1977), p. 125. Some of the wording of my discussion also follows Hill. A detailed examination of the two editions of this tract (the first is more impassioned) is given in E. M. W. Tillyard, *Milton,* rev. ed. (New York: Barnes & Noble, 1967), pp. 119-29.

27. The central importance of shadow to the effect of *Paradise Lost* is found not only in the commanding figure of Satan; the notion of

"shadow" itself is threaded throughout the poem, not only as an opposite to light, but as a foreshadowing of the possibility of salvation through conflict, as when Raphael prefaces his account of the war in heaven with the question,

> . . . what if Earth
> Be but the shadow of Heav'n, and things therein
> Each to other like, more than on Earth is thought?
> —*Paradise Lost,* V (lines 574–76)

See William G. Madsen, "Earth the Shadow of Heaven: Typological Symbolism in *Paradise Lost,*" in *Milton: Modern Essays in Criticism,* ed. A. E. Barker (New York: Oxford University Press, 1965), pp. 246–63.

The poem itself works on the shadow of the reader, since "Milton's method is to re-create in the mind of the reader (which is, finally the poem's scene) the drama of the Fall, to make him fall again exactly as Adam did and with Adam's troubled clarity, that is to say, 'not deceived.'" Stanley E. Fish, *Surprised by Sin: The Reader in Paradise Lost* (Berkeley: University of California Press, 1971), p. 1. As Fish demonstrates, "Milton consciously wants to worry the reader, to force him to doubt the correctness of his responses, and to bring him to the realization that his inability to read the poem with any confidence in his own perception is its focus" (p. 4). This rhetorical strategy is consonant with his moral purpose, which "is to educate the reader to an awareness of his position and responsibilities as a fallen man, and to a sense of the distance which separates him from the innocence once his" (p. 1). As the reader of this chapter will recognize, this is nothing less than the education of integrity through the experience of shadow.

28. Milton, "Cyriack, this three years' day these eyes, though clear," in Davies, *Selected Shorter Poems and Prose,* p. 148.

29. J. Richardson, Father and Son, "Explanatory Notes and Remarks on Milton's Paradise Lost . . ." (London: J. R. Sen, 1734), quoted in Edward Wagenknecht, *The Personality of Milton* (Norman: University of Oklahoma Press, 1970), p. 157.

30. John Milton, *Paradise Lost* (Indianapolis: Bobbs-Merrill, 1962), IX (lines 322–29), p. 211.

31. It was associated in Milton's time with the Dutch Reformed theologian Jacobus Arminius (1560–1609), who asserted, in "a liberal reaction to the Calvinist doctrine of predestination," a "conditional election, according to which God elects to life those who will respond in faith to the divine offer of salvation." "Arminianism" and "Arminius, Jacobus," *The New Encyclopædia Brittanica* (1987), Micropædia vol. 1, p. 569.

32. Douglas Bush, "*Paradise Lost* in Our Time: Religious and Ethical Principles," in *Milton: Modern Essays in Criticism,* ed. Arthur E. Barker (New York: Oxford University Press, 1965), pp. 156–76.

33. C. G. Jung, "A Psychological View of Conscience," in *Civilization in Transition,* Vol. 10, 2nd ed., of *Collected Works* (Princeton, N.J.: Princeton University Press, 1970), pp. 437–55.

34. James Thorpe, *John Milton: The Inner Life* (San Marino, Calif.: Huntington Library, 1983), p. 9.

35. John Milton, *Paradise Lost,* I (lines 17–25), p. 6.

36. John Milton, "Tractate on Education," in *The Prose Works of John Milton,* ed. J. A. St. John (London: H. G. Bohn, 1848–53), vol. 3, p. 464, quoted in Basil Willey, *The Seventeenth Century Background* (New York: Columbia University Press, 1958), p. 243.

37. "God himself is truth, and the more honest anyone is in teaching truth to man, the more like God, and the more acceptable to God, he must be. It is blasphemous to believe that God is jealous of truth, that he does not wish it spread freely among mankind." John Milton, *Second Defence of the English People,* trans. Douglas Bush in *The Portable Milton,* p. 206.

38. Thorpe, *John Milton,* pp. 3, 7.

39. Davies, Introduction, in *John Milton: Selected Shorter Poems and Prose Writings,* pp. 13, 19. Karl Marx's comment is in his *Theories of Surplus Value* (Moscow: Progress, 1975), p. 401. Eliot's comment is found in the chapter entitled "Notes on the Blank Verse of Christopher Marlowe," in his book *The Sacred Wood* (New York: Barnes and Noble, 1960), p. 87.

40. John Milton, "A Masque Presented at Ludlow Castle," 1634, in Davies, *John Milton: Selected Shorter Poems and Prose Writings* (lines 762–73), pp. 48–49.

41. Heinrich Boll, "Courtesy towards God," in Jan Vladislav, ed., *Vaclav Havel or Living in Truth* (London: Faber and Faber, 1989), pp. 210, 211.

42. Pavel Kohout, "The Chaste Centaur," in Vladislav, *Vaclav Havel,* pp. 245–49.

43. Marina Warner, *Monuments and Maidens* (New York: Atheneum, 1985), pp. 241–42.

44. Ibid., p. 242.

45. Josef Pieper, *Prudence,* trans. Richard Winston and Clara Winston (New York: Pantheon Books, 1959), p. 42.

46. Ibid., p. 5.

47. Campbell, "Creativity," p. 142; Eco, *Aesthetics of Aquinas,* pp. 98–102.

48. ". . . he who would not be frustrate of his hope to write well hereafter in laudable things, ought himself to be a true poem, that is, a composition and pattern of the best and honorablest things. . . ." John Milton, "An Apology for Smectymnuus," in Bush, *The Portable Milton,* pp. 132–33.

49. *Trouthe* was the English word used in Chaucer's time for the purity of intent (sadly lacking in most of the society depicted in *The Canterbury Tales*), which could allow a human being to return to moral stability and achieve liberation from mutability, corruption, and death. George Kane, *The Liberating Truth: The Concept of Integrity in Chaucer's Writings* (London: Athlone Press, 1980).

50. James Henry Breasted, *The Dawn of Conscience* (New York: Charles Scribner's, 1933).

51. Boll, "Courtesy towards God," p. 211.

52. Andrew Samuels, "Original Morality in a Depressed Culture," in Mary Ann Mattoon, ed., *The Archetype of Shadow in a Split World,* Proceedings of the Tenth International Congress of Analytical Psychology, Berlin, 1986, (Einsiedeln, Switzerland: Daimon Verlag, 1987), p. 71.

53. "Day of Atonement Part 1, Evening Service," in *Service of the Synagogue* (London: Routledge and Sons, 1904), p. 15.

54. Samuels, "Original Morality," pp. 74, 75.

55. Ibid., pp. 69–83, quotes p. 70. See also my "Discussion," pp.

84-89. An expanded version of Samuels's essay appears as Chapter
11 of his *The Plural Psyche* (London: Routledge, 1989).

56. John Milton, *Paradise Lost,* XI (lines 1086-92), p. 264.

57. Richard Wilhelm in *I Ching,* trans. Wilhelm/Baynes, p. 54.

58. Doris Lessing, *The Four-Gated City* (New York: Knopf, 1969),
pp. 198-99.

59. "McCarthy, Joseph R(aymond)," *The New Encyclopædia Brittanica* (1987), Micropædia vol. 7, p. 611.

60. Ibid.

61. Donald L. Nathanson, ed., *The Many Faces of Shame* (New
York: Guilford Press, 1987). The first major Jungian paper on shame
was also published in 1987: Peer Hultberg, "Shame: An Overshadowed Emotion" in Mattoon, *Archetype of Shadow,* pp. 157-73.

62. In a useful review of the literature, Francis Broucek tells us that
this distinguishing formulation originated with Gerhart Piers, who
"saw guilt as having to do with transgression and shame with failure.
According to Piers, the unconscious threat in shame was abandonment, in guilt castration. Piers also described shame-guilt cycles. . . ."
Broucek, *Shame and the Self* (New York: Guilford Press, 1991), p. 13.
See also G. Piers and M. Singer, *Shame and Guilt* (Springfield, Ill.:
C C Thomas, 1953).

63. Erik H. Erikson, *Childhood and Society,* 2nd ed. (New York:
W. W. Norton, 1963), p. 252.

64. Ibid., p. 253.

65. Erich Neumann, *The Origins and History of Consciousness* (New
York: Pantheon Books, 1954); Joseph Henderson, *Thresholds of Initiation* (Middletown, Conn.: Wesleyan University Press, 1967); Marie-Louise von Franz, *A Psychological Interpretation of the Golden Ass of
Apuleius* (New York: Spring Publications, 1970).

66. Heinz Kohut, *The Restoration of the Self* (New York: International Universities Press, 1977).

67. Andrew P. Morrison, "The Eye Turned Inward: Shame and
the Self" in Nathanson, *The Many Faces of Shame,* pp. 271-91.

68. An implication of this formulation is that failure to connect
with an idealized father will often lead to shame, and that the mother

will seem negative to the extent that she comes between a child and this goal.

69. Gabriele Taylor, *Pride, Shame, and Guilt* (Oxford: Clarendon Press, 1985), p. 134.

70. Erikson, *Childhood and Society,* p. 253.

71. Taylor, *Pride, Shame, and Guilt,* pp. 134–35.

72. Andrew P. Morrison, "Shame and the Psychology of the Self" in *Kohut's Legacy: Contributions to Self Psychology,* ed. Paul Stepansky and Arnold Goldberg (Hillsdale, N.J.: Analytic Press, 1984), pp. 71–90. Morrison includes "within the designation 'shame' those related phenomena of humiliation, mortification, remorse, apathy, embarrassment, and lowered self-esteem" (p. 71). Shame is described as "the subjectively experienced defeat of the self in the pursuit of its goals" (p. 82).

73. Francis Broucek regards "the sense of shame" as a "discretionary function that makes us pause before doing something that would arouse the painful feeling of shame in ourselves or another." He notes that "the clinical literature on shame is focused on shame as affect and usually fails to recognize the concept of the sense of shame as the safeguard of our psychic life." *Shame and the Self,* p. 5. Broucek (p. 5) cites Carl Schneider's *Shame, Exposure, and Privacy* (Boston: Beacon Press, 1977) as an exception that distinguished "the sense of shame and an actual shame experience" and "emphasized how vital is the sense of shame to our individual and collective emotional, moral, and spiritual welfare."

74. Mary Douglas, *Purity and Danger: An Analysis of the Concepts of Pollution and Taboo* (London: Ark, 1984), p. 159. Obviously, this process can have tragically confusing results when applied to persons, as we have seen with the treatment of women throughout Judeo-Christian culture. My analytic reading of Douglas focuses on the positive aspect of pollution concepts when they are applied to intrapsychic rituals rather than made the basis of externalizing projections.

75. In this essay he says, "We can speak of the Mass as *the rite of the individuation process.*" C. G. Jung, "Transformation Symbolism in the Mass," (1941/1954), in *Psychology and Religion: West and East,*

NOTES TO PAGES 68-75

Vol. II, 2nd ed., of *Collected Works* (Princeton, N.J.: Princeton University Press, 1969), p. 273, para. 414.

76. Patricia Berry, "Virginities of Image," in Joanne Stroud and Gail Thomas, eds., *Images of the Untouched* (Dallas: Spring Publications, 1982), p. 37.

77. William Butler Yeats, *Selected Poems and Three Plays,* 3rd ed., ed. M. L. Rosenthal (1962; New York: Macmillan, Collier Books, 1986), p. 199.

78. Berry, "Virginities of Image," p. 38.

CHAPTER 3. INTEGRITY AND GENDER

1. Alasdair MacIntyre, *After Virtue,* 2nd ed. (Notre Dame, Ind.: University of Notre Dame Press, 1984), p. 181.

2. Ibid., Chapter 14, "The Nature of the Virtues," pp. 180–203.

3. Nancy Hale, *The Realities of Fiction* (London: MacMillan, 1963), p. 69. Hale quotes Frank O'Connor's remark, "I have small doubt that the subject of a novel is almost invariably the relation of the individual to society."

4. Barbara Stevens Sullivan, *Psychotherapy Grounded in the Feminine Principle* (Wilmette, Ill.: Chiron Publications, 1989).

5. I would suggest that the reader interested in this point peruse the next-to-last chapter of the novel. Jane Austen, *Persuasion* (New York: Bantam, 1984), pp. 207–10.

6. This is the hypothesis that the earth is a living organism, called Gaia in honor of the Greek primordial earth goddess, who, as Christine Downing puts it, "differs from the later goddesses in that she *is*—and remains, earth, earth recognized as animate and divine." *The Goddess* (New York: Crossroad, 1984), p. 140.

7. MacIntyre, *After Virtue,* p. 203.

8. Ibid., p. 183.

9. Ibid., p. 240.

10. Ibid., p. 203.

11. Ibid., p. 240. This was the third Earl of Shaftesbury, Anthony Ashley Cooper, 1671–1713. According to a recent biography of Aus-

ten, a popular work of his was "*Characteristics of Men, Manners, Opinions, Times* (1711), in which happiness was said to be possible for those who heed promptings of virtue and act on their instinctive benevolence. Morality, in this view, depends on 'heart' and not on 'head', and though Shaftesbury does not deny our rational access to truth he encourages partisans of 'heart'" (Park Honan, *Jane Austen: Her Life* [New York: Fawcett Columbine, 1987], p. 276). But Honan notes that *Persuasion* counters the philosophy of Shaftesbury, who had "judged a moral action partly by its effects" and supports "the tough eighteenth-century rationalism of Joseph Butler" who "held that the consequences of any action have nothing to do with its basic rightness" (pp. 383-84).

12. MacIntyre, *After Virtue*, pp. 241-42.

13. Ibid., p. 242.

14. Jung writes, "Careful investigation has shown that the affective character of a man has feminine traits. From this psychological fact derives . . . my own concept of the anima. Deeper introspection or ecstatic experience reveals the existence of a feminine figure in the unconscious, hence the feminine name: anima, psyche, *Seele.*" Jung, "Commentary on 'The Secret of the Golden Flower,'" in *Alchemical Studies*, Vol. 13 of *Collected Works* (Princeton, N.J.: Princeton University Press, 1967), pp. 39-40, para. 58. Just as there are many affective natures, there are many styles of anima, each having a different character and strength of moral disposition. In projection these anima styles can become demands placed on women to incarnate certain qualities.

15. Warner, *Monuments and Maidens*, pp. 249-50.

16. C. G. Jung, "Commentary on 'The Secret of the Golden Flower'", pp. 15-16, para. 18.

17. Sissela Bok, *Lying: Moral Choice in Public and Private Life* (New York: Vintage Books, 1978), pp. 285-90.

18. Carol Gilligan, *In a Different Voice* (Cambridge: Harvard University Press, 1982); Carol Gilligan, Janie Victoria Ward, and Jill McLean Taylor with Betty Bardige, eds., *Mapping the Moral Domain* (Cambridge: Harvard University Press, 1988); Carol Gilligan, Nona P. Lyons,

and Trudy Hanmer, eds., *Making Connections* (Cambridge: Harvard University Press, 1990).

19. The only English-language rendering of Jung's original 1912 version of this book is *Psychology of the Unconscious,* trans. Beatrice M. Hinkle (New York: Dodd, Mead, 1916). Taken simply as a study of the mother image, Jung's book was not novel. Its first part met with Freud's approval as a welcome addition to the growing literature on the mother complex, which by 1911 included Freud's monograph *Leonardo da Vinci: A Psychosexual Study of an Infantile Reminiscence* (New York: Moffat Yard, 1916) and Karl Abraham's "Giovanni Segantini: A Psychoanalytic Study" in his *Clinical Papers and Essays on Psychoanalysis* (New York: Basic Books, 1955), pp. 210–61. Moreover, Jung initially represents the regressing libido in patriarchal terms as a hero approaching the unconscious, which is depicted as a negative mother dragon guarding the treasure of new consciousness (Sonu Shamdasani, personal communication).

20. Jung later told colleagues that he had emphasized the mother so much in *Wandlungen und Symbole der Libido* to compensate for Freud's heavy emphasis on the father (Joseph Henderson, personal communication).

21. Sonu Shamdasani points out that the last straw for Freud was Jung's blatant acceptance of teleology, which he put forth in Christian terms as the idea that the patient's regression to the mother was serving a spiritual goal. Shamdasani also notes that Jung was not alone in wanting to broaden the ethical basis of psychoanalysis by introducing philosophical ideas. For example, see James J. Putnam, "A Plea for the Study of Philosophic Methods in Preparation for Psychoanalytic Work," in *Addresses on Psycho-Analysis* (London: Hogarth Press, 1951), pp. 79–96.

22. C. G. Jung, *Memories, Dreams, Reflections* (New York: Pantheon Books, 1963), p. 150.

23. Joseph Henderson, personal communication.

24. Jung, *Memories, Dreams, Reflections,* pp. 48–50. The notes for these pages, quoting from Jung's then unpublished "Seminar on *Interpretation of Visions,*" tell us that for Jung the "natural mind" is the

"mind which says absolutely straight and ruthless things," and that it "is the sort of mind which springs from natural sources, and not from opinions taken from books; it wells up from the earth like a natural spring, and brings with it the peculiar wisdom of nature." In his autobiography, Jung goes on to say: "I too have this archaic nature, and in me it is linked with the gift—not always pleasant— of seeing people and things as they are. I can let myself be deceived from here to Tipperary when I don't want to recognize something, and yet at bottom I know quite well how matters really stand. In this I am like a dog—he can be tricked, but he always smells it out in the end. This 'insight' is based on instinct, or on a *'participation mystique'* with others. It is as if the 'eyes of the background' do the seeing in an impersonal act of perception." Ibid., p. 50.

25. Ibid., p. 48.

26. Ibid., p. 8.

27. Jeffrey Satinover, "At the Mercy of Another: Abandonment and Restitution in Psychosis and Psychotic Character," *Chiron: A Review of Jungian Analysis* (1985): 47–86.

28. Jung, *Two Essays,* p. 240, para. 405.

29. *I Ching,* trans. Wilhelm/Baynes, p. 13.

30. N. J. Girardot, *Myth and Meaning in Early Taoism* (Berkeley: University of California Press, 1983), p. 56, Chinese supplied by Girardot. (The translation of Lao Tzu is based on that of Chiang Hsich'ang and that of Wing-tsit Chan.)

31. Ibid., p. 56.

32. Ibid., p. 61.

33. See John Layard, *The Virgin Archetype* (New York: Spring Publications, 1972).

34. For example, Joseph Henderson's "C. G. Jung: A Reminiscent Picture of His Method," *Journal of Analytical Psychology* 20/2 (1975): 114–21.

35. Laurens van der Post, *Jung and the Story of Our Time* (New York: Pantheon Books, 1975), pp. 57–58.

36. Elizabeth Osterman, personal communication.

37. According to Plutarch, "as Romulus was casting up a ditch,

where he designed the foundation of the city-wall [Remus, feeling that Romulus had cheated in a contest as to where the city's site should be] turned some pieces of the work to ridicule, and obstructed others; at last, as he was in contempt leaping over it, some say Romulus himself struck him. . . ." *Plutarch's Lives,* trans. John Dryden and rev. Arthur Hugh Clough (New York: Modern Library, 1967), p. 30. Comparing the two, Plutarch says, "They both proved brave and manly. . . . But Romulus seemed rather to act by counsel, and to show the sagacity of a statesman, and in all his dealings with their neighbors, whether relating to feeding of flocks or to hunting, gave the idea of being born rather to rule than to obey." Ibid., p. 27.

38. Adrienne Rich, "Integrity," in *A Wild Patience Has Taken Me This Far: Poems, 1978–1981* (New York: W. W. Norton, 1981), p. 9.

39. Jolande Jacobi interview, pp. 42–43, C. G. Jung Biographical Archive, Countway Library of Medicine, Harvard Medical School, Boston, Massachusetts. Jacobi says that Jung told her that the seduction that occurred was by one of the best friends of his family.

40. Jung, *Memories, Dreams, Reflections,* p. 12.

41. I have written elsewhere that this dream demonstrates that Hermes was Jung's guiding mythologem, since the phallos is obviously a Herm: C. G. Jung, *Aspects of the Masculine,* ed. John Beebe (Princeton, N.J.: Princeton University Press, 1989), p. xvii. But the mythological association of Hermes and Apollo is well known, and though Jung's psychological creativity was guided by Hermes, his astrological sign was Leo, whose ruler is the Sun, and he had also an enormous, though rarely acknowledged, power-drive.

42. Howard Teich, "Homovision; the Solar/Lunar Twin-Ego," unpublished.

43. Jung discovered, in his researches, that the alchemical formula for the development of luna, the feminine principle, was salt and mercury, and for the development of sol, the masculine principle, was sulphur and mercury. He knew that Mercurius was duplex and imaged as the monoculus, a union of male figures. (C. G. Jung, *Mysterium Coniunctionis,* Vol. 14 of *Collected Works* [Princeton, N.J.: Princeton University Press, 1963], plates 4 and 5.) He also uncovered a white

sulphur and a red sulphur. He writes: "Red sulphur stands for the masculine, active principle of the sun, the white for that of the moon. As sulphur is generally masculine by nature and forms the counterpart of the feminine salt, the two figures probably signify the spirits of the arcane substance, which is often called rex. . . ." (Ibid., pp. 506–507, para. 720). On the basis of this passage, Teich (personal communication) believes that the red sulphur signifies solar masculinity and the white sulphur lunar masculinity. He suggests that the monoculus may also be interpreted as representing the union of these two sulphurs, a union of male opposites, which, in combination with mercury, produces the mature masculine principle that can go on to unite with the feminine principle.

44. Murray Stein, "A Polarity in Conscience: Solar and Lunar Aspects," Diploma thesis, C. G. Jung Institut–Zurich, 1973. Stein finds the dialogue between solar and lunar conscience in the Homeric Hymn to Zeus (in the image of Zeus and the Titaness Themis) and in the Old Testament (in the myth of the relationship of Yahweh and Sophia [Proverbs 8]). Solar conscience "extracts laws and norms" from the archetype dominant in the conscious attitude of the individual and in the collective consciousness of the society at large, speaking generally "for custom, cultural habits, social laws and expectations and for a group ethic. . . . It has a particular gift for elevating such norms into ideals of a highly abstract nature, ideals such as truthfulness, justice, purity" (pp. 22–24). Lunar conscience, by contrast "turns away from cultural and social dominants in the human environment as the source of the value-contents of conscience, to nature and instinct as their source, away from the steady certainties of right and wrong as laid down by the dominant archetype and codified in bodies of law, to the fluctuations of doubt in reflection and some odd paradoxes in certain ethical compulsions; away from a kind of conscience that would force the ego into the narrow trail of moral perfection, to a sort of conscience that insists on wholeness and completeness; away from a love of law, to a law of love" (Stein, p. 54).

45. David Tacey, "Attacking Patriarchy, Redeeming Masculinity," *San Francisco Jung Institute Library Journal* 10/1 (1991): 25–41.

CHAPTER 4. WORKING ON INTEGRITY

1. Willeford, *Feeling, Imagination, and Self,* p. 28.

2. Lionel Trilling, *Sincerity and Authenticity* (Cambridge: Harvard University Press, 1972), p. 3.

3. O. Hobart Mowrer, "Integrity Therapy: A Self-Help Approach," *Psychotherapy: Theory, Research & Practice* 3/1 (1966): 114–19; O. Hobart Mowrer, "A Revolution in Integrity?" *Voices* 3/1 (1967): 26–33.

4. Karl Menninger, *Whatever Became of Sin?* (New York: Hawthorn, 1973).

5. Leo Rangell, "A Psychoanalytic Perspective Leading Currently to the Syndrome of the Compromise of Integrity," *International Journal of Psychoanalysis* 55 (1974): 3–12.

6. Lewis M. Andrews, *To Thine Own Self Be True* (New York: Doubleday, 1989).

7. Hamlet even thinks at first that he has killed the more blatant representative of the mother's animus, Claudius.

8. Erich Neumann, *The Origins and History of Consciousness* (New York: Pantheon Books, 1954); Joseph Henderson, *Thresholds of Initiation* (Middletown, Conn.: Wesleyan University Press, 1967).

9. James Hillman, *Anima: An Anatomy of a Personified Notion* (Dallas: Spring Publications, 1985).

10. Marie-Louise von Franz, "The Inferior Function," in *Lectures on Jung's Typology* (Dallas: Spring Publications, 1971).

11. Ibid., p. 56.

12. In this patient, who is an introverted feeling type, the animus would have the character of inferior extraverted thinking.

13. This was probably a "lunar" man, who could receive my ideas. I think the insight also involved her superior function, illuminated by the burst of solar femininity into a clearer recognition of her own nature. Using the language of Chinese philosophy, Genia Haddon has described the kind of self-assertion that this patient displayed in coming to her insight as "yang femininity." See her article, "Delivering Yang Femininity," *Spring* (1987): 133–42.

14. James Hillman, *The Dream and the Underworld* (New York: Harper and Row, 1979).

15. "The *vas bene clausum* (well-sealed vessel) is a precautionary measure very frequently mentioned in alchemy, and is the equivalent of the magic circle. In both cases the idea is to protect what is within from the intrusion and admixture of what is without, as well as to prevent it from escaping." C. G. Jung, *Psychology and Alchemy,* Vol. 12, 2nd ed., of *Collected Works* (Princeton, N.J.: Princeton University Press, 1968), p. 167, para. 219.

16. "This term simply expresses the fact that the outward situation releases a psychic process in which certain contents gather together and prepare for action. When we say that a person is 'constellated' we mean that he has taken up a position from which he can be expected to react in a quite definite way." C. G. Jung, "A Review of the Complex Theory," in *The Structure and Dynamics of the Psyche,* Vol. 8 of *Collected Works* (Princeton, N.J.: Princeton University Press, 1960), p. 94, para. 198.

17. "The Three Surgeons," in *Grimms' Tales for Young and Old,* trans. Ralph Manheim (New York: Doubleday, 1977), pp. 404–406. This story is called "The Three Army Surgeons" in the Grimms' original.

18. He made this statement in an interview which I am quoting from memory.

19. Samuel Sambursky, *Physics of the Stoics* (Westport, Conn.: Greenwood Press, 1973), p. 7.

20. Ibid., p. 1.

21. There is also a Christian implication. Marina Warner has noted that a jar of precious ointment "clasped between her reformed hands" is a traditional "iconographical attribute" of Mary Magdalen, implying, like the sieve of Tuccia, that "a virtuous body must appear a sound, watertight container." This is another image of integrity, containing healing power. "[T]he perfumed and costly oil within was linked with the 'love' to which Jesus referred when he defended the Magdalen against the apostles." Warner, *Monuments and Maidens,* p. 257 and plate 71.

154

22. Jung, "Commentary on 'Golden Flower,'" p. 16, para. 20.

23. Her immaturity illustrates (once again) the traditional failure of gender integrity in our civilization. Ridiculously "lunar," the love-struck serving maid shows no trace of "solar" discrimination. The soldier who steals body parts at night seems, by contrast, a sinister lunar shadow that this one-sided anima figure cannot resist. This has been a common imbalance in the unconscious of people in our culture.

EPILOGUE

1. St. Thomas Aquinas, *Summa Contra Gentiles*, I, 30, quoted in Antonin G. Sertillanges, *Foundations of Thomistic Philosophy*, trans. Godfrey Anstruther (Springfield, Ill.: Templegate, 1956), p. 92.

2. Erik H. Erikson, "The Integrative Values of the Human Life Cycle," Sophia Mirviss Memorial Lecture, Jan. 5, 1960, typescript, San Francisco Psychoanalytic Society & Institute and Mount Zion Hospital & Medical Center, pp. 27–28.

Index

idealized parental imago, 63; betrayal of, 66
image, 6, 114. *See also* integrity,
image of
impurity, 68–69
Indian philosophy, 115
individuation, 22, 43, 47; Havel's,
50; Jung's, 78–80, 94, 97–98;
Mass as rite of, 145n75; Milton's,
45; in *Persuasion,* 73, 92
inferior function, 106–107
integration, xi; of shadow, 33
integrative power of the psyche, 115
integritas, 6, 13, 16, 54, 68, 125,
131n22
integrity: as alternative to despair,
126; capacity to promote, 122,
153n21; in Chinese philosophy,
27–32, 38–39, 59–60, 88–89,
136n48; compromise of, 33, 40,
100, 123; construction of, 114–15;
culture of, 42; in danger, 33; de-
fined, 3, 17, 22, 32; as desideratum, 15; as ecological sense, 32;
education of, 48; etymology of,
6; in fiction, 71, 72–73; of gender, 98; of life, as art, 54, 143n48;
modern understanding of, 46;
need for, in masculinity, 95–98;
and obligation, 34; particular vs.
ideal, 23; patriarchal definitions
of, 86; persona, 100–102; psychotherapist's, 19–21, 133n32; relationship necessary for, 123–24;
and responsibility, 3; as sensitivity
to needs of whole, 32, 125–26;
shared field of, 19; symptoms of,
34–36, 40, 69; as *te,* 29–32; and
therapy, 100; and *Virginitas,* 77–
78; as virtue, 70, 140n23; virtues
of, 131n23; as word, 5, 16–17, 46,
54–55

————, feminine style of, 73–74;
in Austen, 72–76, 97–98; in Gilligan, 80–81; in Jung, 78–80; as
twinship, 92
————, image of: and absence of
personification, 43, 140n23; repressed, 40–41, 140n23; sieve of
Tuccia as, 50–53; Taoist, 89
Integrity: A Philosophical Inquiry
(Halfon), 131n23
intersubjectivity, 19, 132n30
intimacy: through shame, 66–67
intuition, 22, 24–27, 134–35n36; as
auxiliary function, 106
irrational functions, 24–26, 134–
35n36
Isakower, 41

Jacobi, Jolande, 150n39
James, Henry, 72
Jane Austen: Her Life (Honan),
147n11
Jesus, 43–44
Joan of Arc (Warner), 76
John Milton: The Inner Life
(Thorpe), 47–48
John of the Cross, 18
Johnson, Samuel, *Life of Milton,* 42
Joyce, James, *Portrait of the Artist as
a Young Man,* 131n22
Judaism, 56–57
Julius Caesar, 128n11
Jung, C. G., 18, 32, 45, 52, 72;
centrality of integrity in work of,
27, 133n30, 134n32; on facing the
shadow, 33, 35; feminine figures
in adult development of, 78; and
matriarchal ethic for psychotherapy, 81–82, 148n19; own mother
in childhood of, 84–86; on psychological types, 20–21, 24, 105–
106; on the Self, 49, 74, 79,

Jung, C. G. (*cont.*)
135n41; style of masculinity of,
90–92, 94–98
————, works of: *Alchemical
Studies,* 79–80, 147n14; *Civilization in Transition,* 47, 142n33;
"Commentary on 'The Secret of
the Golden Flower,'" 122; *Letters,*
36; *Memories, Dreams, Reflections,*
84–85, 92–93, 148–49n24; *Practice
of Psychotherapy,* 40; *Psychological
Types,* 22–23, 27–28; *Psychology
and Alchemy,* 153n15; *Structure and
Dynamics of the Psyche,* 153n16;
"Transformation Symbolism in
the Mass," 67, 145n75; *Two Essays,* 87–88; *Wandlungen and Symbole der Libido,* 82–84, 148n20,
148n21
Jung, Emma, 83, 95
justice, 80–81
justification, 34, 47

Kant, Immanuel, 80
karma, 30
Kierkegaard, Soren Aabye, *Enten-
Eller,* 76
Kohut, Heinz, 19, 37, 133n30; *Res-
toration of the Self,* 63–64

Lacan, Jacques, 81
Laing, Ronald, quoted, 119
Langs, Robert, 19
Lao Tzu, 123; *Tao Tê Ching,* 28–30,
89
La Rochefoucauld, François de, 118
Lessing, Doris, *Four-Gated City,* 60
Letters: of Jung, 36; of Seneca, 14–15
Levinas, Emmanuel, *Levinas Reader,*
33–35
Liberalism, 41, 48
libido, 89

Life of Milton (Johnson), 42
limitation, 22, 50
Lincoln, Abraham, 123
logos, 18, 81, 86, 90
luna, 86, 91, 150n43
lunar, the, 91–95; and conscience,
96; energies of, 94; as shadow
figure, 154n23; in woman, 106,
152n13
lunar femininity, 154n23
lunar masculinity, 93–95, 97–98,
104; as white sulphur, 151n43

McCarthy, Joseph, 60–61
Machiavelli, Niccolo, *Prince,* 36
Machiavellianism, 58
MacIntyre, Alasdair, *After Virtue,*
70, 74–76
McMorran, Ian, quoted, 136n48
Madonna (pop star), 48–49
Mair, Victor, 136n45; quoted, 29–
30
mandala, 74, 113
manipulation, 64
Marx, Karl, *Theories of Surplus
Value,* 48, 59
Marxism, 42
masculine, 72, 86, 91, 94, 150–
51n43
masculinity, 92; Jung's, 90–94. *See
also* lunar masculinity; solar
masculinity
Maslow, Abraham, 133n30
Masson, Jeffrey Moussaieff, 19
matriarchal psychology, 81–84;
Jung and, 85–86
Ma-wang-tui manuscripts, 29–30,
121, 136n45
Mead, George Herbert, 132n30
Memorabilia (Xenophon), 13
Memories, Dreams, Reflections
(Jung), 84–85, 92–93, 148–49n24

On Duties (Panaetius), 14, 129–30n19
On Poetry and Poets (Eliot), 42, 139n18
oral stage of development, 64
original morality, 56–58
other, Levinas's concept of, 34

Panaetius, On Duties, 14, 129–30n19
Paradise Lost (Milton), 45–48, 56, 58–59, 140–41n27
Paradise Regained (Milton), 47
paradoxes of dream interpretation, 111–14
participation, 32, 132n30
Pascal, Blaise, Pensees, 23, 135n37
patriarchy, 84, 101–102
penitence, 66. See also contrition
Pensees (Pascal), 23, 135n37
Perls, Fritz, 110
persona, 97, 100–102
Persuasion (Austen), 72–74, 76–77
philosophy. See Chinese philosophy; Indian philosophy; moral philosophy; Stoic philosophy; individual philosophers
Pieper, Josef, Prudence, 53–54
Piers, Gerhart, 144n62
Plato, 139n15; Republic, 36
pleasure, 19, 132n27, 133n30
Pliny, Natural History, 51
Plutarch, 149–50n37
pneuma, 122
political imagery, 36, 40, 100–101
pollution, 67, 145n74
Polonius, 81, 99–102
Pompey, 128n11
Portrait of the Artist as a Young Man (Joyce), 131n2
Practice of Psychotherapy, The (Jung), 40
Preiswerk, Helly, 78

pre-Oedipal stage of development, 61–63
pride, 7, 10, 64, 96
Pride, Shame, and Guilt (Taylor), 64
Prince, The (Machiavelli), 36
projection, 50, 76–77, 95–96
prudence, 53–54, 55
Prudence (Pieper), 53–54
"Psychic Activity of Dreaming, The" (Henderson), 24–27
psychological types, 21–22, 24–27, 134–35n36; in working on integrity, 105–109, 152n12
Psychological Types (Jung), 22–23, 27–28
Psychology and Alchemy (Jung), 153n15
psychotherapy, 19–21, 34, 69; case examples from, 26–27, 102–109, 109–15; as feminine, 72; relationship of, in dreams, 112
Psychotherapy Grounded in the Feminine Principle (Sullivan), 72
Puritanism, 41–44, 66, 69, 70; duty toward self in, 43; post-traumatic reaction to, 41–42, 139n18; resurgence of, in psychotherapy, 49; as superego perversion, 44, 140n24
Puritan Smile, The (Neville), 41–42, 139n15
purity: archetype of, 44, 55, 57; as ideal, 49; sacred, 67
Purity and Danger (Douglas), 67, 145n74

rage, 124; Hamlet's, 102; in psychotherapy, 20–21, 66, 103–108
Rangell, Leo: Mind of Watergate, 40; quoted, 100
Rank, Otto, 133n30
rational functions, 23, 134–35n36

Integrity in Depth was composed into type on a Compugraphic digital phototypesetter in twelve point Bembo with two points of spacing between the lines. Bembo was also selected for display. The book was designed by Jim Billingsley, typeset by Metricomp, Inc., printed offset by Thomson-Shore, Inc., and bound by John H. Dekker & Sons, Inc. The paper on which this book is printed carries acid-free characteristics for an effective life of at least three hundred years.

TEXAS A&M UNIVERSITY PRESS
College Station